www.a… ion

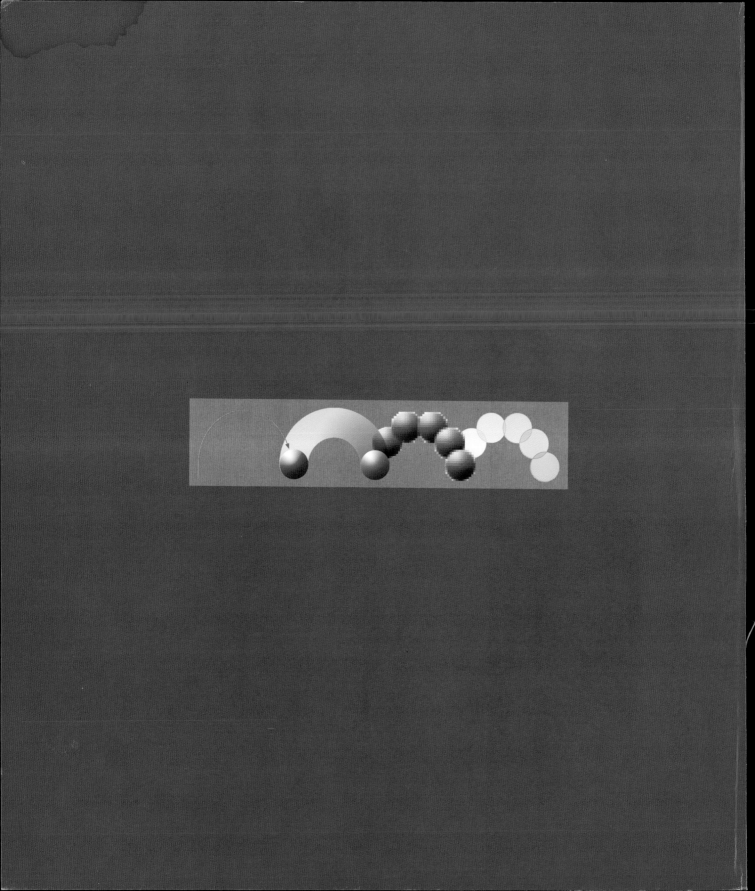

www.animation

JENNY CHAPMAN

SERIES CONSULTANT
ALASTAIR CAMPBELL

WATSON-GUPTILL
PUBLICATIONS
New York

This book was conceived, designed, and produced by The Ilex Press Limited, The Barn, College Farm, 1 West End, Whittlesford, Cambridge, CB2 4LX

Sales and Editorial Office
The Old Candlemakers, West Street, Lewes, East Sussex, BN7 2NZ

Publisher: Sophie Collins
Art Director:
Alastair Campbell
Editorial Director:
Steve Luck
Design Manager:
Tony Seddon
Project Editor:
Georga Godwin
Designer: Kevin Knight

ISBN 0-8230-5856-5

Library of Congress Cataloging-in-Publication Data

Chapman, Jenny.
www.animation/Jenny Chapman. p. cm.
Includes bibliographical references and index.
ISBN 0-8230-5856-5
1. Computer animation.
2. Web sites—Design.
I. Title.
TR897.7 .C4322 2001
006.6'96--dc21
2001005476

Originated and printed by Hong Kong Graphics and Printing Ltd., China

The author would like to thank all the artists, designers and companies whose work is featured in this book, and particularly the following people, who have provided special assistance or material: Andy Deck (artcontext Open Studio); Chris Derochie (The Forge Studios Ltd.); Jason Krogh (zinc Roe design); Fatima Laklaty (Ici la lune); James Paterson (presstube); Nathan Pearce (Sony Online Entertainment); Helen Thorington (New Radio and Performing Arts Inc., Turbulence website); Alan Watts (16 color). Special thanks, too, to Charley Surrey of Ivy Press for all her support and assistance.

All Web sites mentioned in this book were current at the time of writing, but due to the changing nature of the Internet, it is possible that some are no longer in existence.

CONTENTS

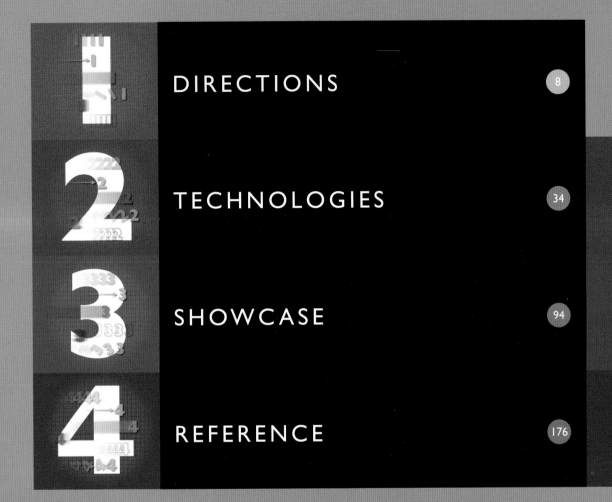

INTRODUCTION

Animation has been with us for a hundred years, but for most of that time it played in isolation from other media, to a passive audience watching a movie or television screen. It had become an established but sedate senior citizen. Suddenly, in the late 1990s, animation was reborn as a vibrant youth. On the Web, computers present still images, text, and sound interwoven with moving images, in a nonlinear and interactive virtual world available to anyone connected to the Internet. So here, animation may be anything from a change in the color of a single button to a full screen display of fast-moving, responsive elements—and it is out there all the time, ready and waiting for interaction. The World Wide Web has shattered the boundaries of animation once and for all, altering its definition, its role, and its future.

An exciting new environment attracts new people, from all kinds of backgrounds. Web animation is being made not only by animators and graphic designers, but by musicians, engineers, and professional skateboarders, to name but a few. This diversity of inspiration has brought a wonderful richness and variety to Web animation design, which is reflected throughout this book.

Jenny Chapman

Archaracle, Scotland

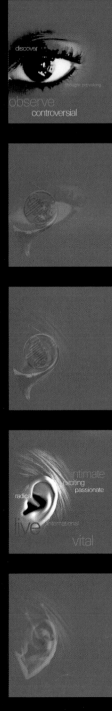
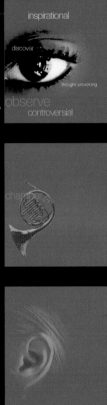

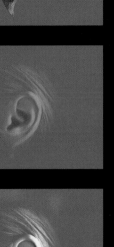
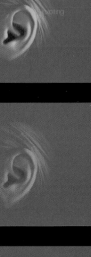

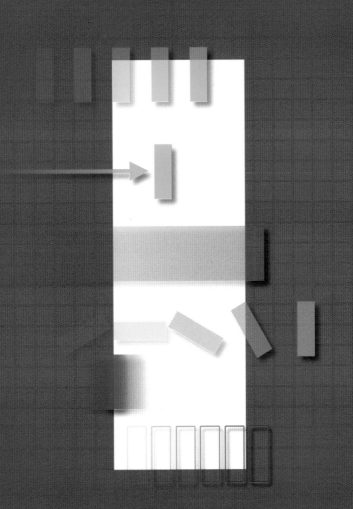

NEW HORIZONS

Until a few years ago, the only way to experiment with animation outside a specialized studio was by using a movie camera with a stop-motion facility. While would-be designers and artists could develop skills in drawing, typography, and design with a minimum of means, any animation more advanced than a flip book required special equipment, dedication, and a certain amount of cash. But with the advent of desktop computing things changed, and by the mid-1990s it was possible to buy a computer capable of some form of animation in many retail outlets. Now infants can create animations on their parents' PCs and see instant results,

and teenagers and aspiring professionals can experiment at home with software that is industry standard. Even with just the most basic freeware or shareware tools, which come free as cover CDs on magazines or on the Internet, it is possible to make professional-looking Web animation in the form of animated GIFs.

The advances in technology that made desktop computers scarcely more expensive than a good-quality TV and video were followed by a phenomenal expansion of access to the World Wide Web, and the development of the Web design industry. But most of the technologies that give the world's top companies a presence on the Web are available in some form to the home user. Now anyone who is prepared to master some basic skills can set up their own Web page at a minimal cost. In this way the Web has been a great leveler—although it is one thing to put up a Web site, and another to persuade people to visit it. Fortunately, there is a network of Web 'zines and similar resources, such as www.linkdup.com, which exist for just that purpose. Any site can be submitted for inclusion: if they think it makes the grade, they will provide a link to it as a public service.

Because this new arena for animation—the World Wide Web—is computer-based, it is possible for it to exploit the power of computation inherent in the technology itself—not only to ensure rapid changes and playback of animation, but to enable user interactivity. This has led to remarkable developments in online games and interactive collaborative work, both for art's sake and just for fun. It could well be said that the World

Wide Web has broadened the horizons for animation more than for any other graphic form. The transition to a virtual environment has provided new opportunities and challenges for every discipline, but typography, static graphics of all kinds, and layout design, for example, all appear in a context that bears a recognizable visual relation to print media. It is not by coincidence that we refer to each part of a Web site as a Web page.

In animation a far more radical change has occurred. With the exception of special cases like flip books, it never had much to do with print media. Animation used to be defined by the silver or the small black screen. On some Web sites, of course, animation is once again king but more frequently it must play one of a myriad of often minor roles, as an integrated element in a much larger whole. The challenge for Web animation designers is to make the most of these new opportunities, and so enable animation to realize its full potential in this new and exciting environment.

1
Sites such as www.linkdup.com provide a valuable service to the creators of Web animation and those looking for inspiration. With their links organized into multiple indexes, it is possible to search by many different categories—or just to look at the latest additions. They even provide a lucky dip, in the form of a changing random selection.

2
Advanced Shockwave interactivity is provided at www.thepowerstation.co.uk in a site celebrating new horizons for both this famous London landmark and Web animation. By moving and clicking the mouse, the kaleidoscopic pattern can be constantly shifted and renewed.

OUTSIDE SOURCES

When designers start creating animated elements for the World Wide Web they are often entering the world of animation for the first time. This is an advantage because they will not be bound by notions of what constitutes animation and how it should work and a disadvantage because they lack training in basic skills.

In many cases the sources used to create the animated elements on Web pages are not drawn from animation history, but the world at large. This is true not only for content, but for the action of the animation itself—the way it moves or behaves. Traditional animation often depended on close observation of the movements of living creatures and natural phenomena. But for the larger arena of Web animation this has often proved to be neither sufficient nor appropriate. Fortunately there are many other sources from which designers can draw their inspiration. Many are visual: from skywriting to juggling to rotating billboards, the world abounds in unnatural, constructed movements. Animation reverse engineers these movements to arrive at the stages out of which they are built—and then rebuilds them again. For the Web we may require just two stages or states—or we may require a long, fluent sequence. The juggler's ball may be here—and then gone. Or we may see the whole path of its travel.

Sometimes people use their own bodies en masse to create an illusion of some greater movement. The Mexican Wave is one of the most crude cases, but there are many more examples, from a synchronized swimming display to the path of fire created on a dark mountainside by a stream of skiers carrying flaming torches. On some designers' Web sites we can drag the mouse across the screen to create a similar wake of movement in its path.

Web animators come from diverse backgrounds, with all kinds of skills and ideas. Music is a common area of inspiration; hardly surprising since musical rhythms, textures, and structures are readily transposed into animated visual form. Other Web animators bring skills in painting, sculpture, engineering, sports, and psychology—almost anything, in fact. When thrown into the melting pot of the World Wide Web, and extracted in a chain of inspiration passing from one designer to another, the result is an amazingly rich and eclectic blend of results.

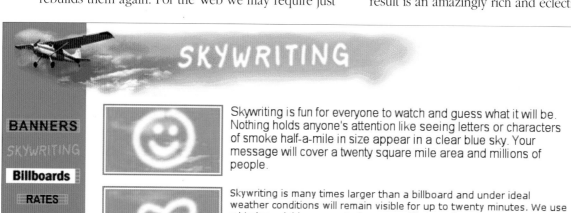

SKYWRITING

Skywriting is fun for everyone to watch and guess what it will be. Nothing holds anyone's attention like seeing letters or characters of smoke half-a-mile in size appear in a clear blue sky. Your message will cover a twenty square mile area and millions of people.

Skywriting is many times larger than a billboard and under ideal weather conditions will remain visible for up to twenty minutes. We use a biodegradable, non-petroleum, paraffin based product to produce vapors that evaporate harmlessly into the atmosphere.

BANNERS
SKYWRITING
Billboards
RATES
EVENTS
HOME

1
Looking at a static screenshot of Adsaloft's Web site, the smiley face and heart could be animated GIFs, in which the symbols draw themselves on the page. In fact they are a series of photos of smoke drawings in the sky, maybe half a mile high.

2

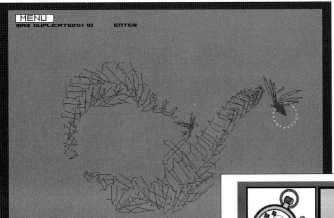

3

FASTBALL REACTION TIME

[If this Shockwave exhibit doesn't load properly, please visit our help page.]

2

Versions of the Archinet piece and other interactive animations at www.presstube.com demonstrate the potential for animation created by duplication of elements in the path of a moving mouse.

3

There are many online "push-button" exhibits at the site of the San Francisco Exploratorium, at www.exploratorium. edu. A click of the mouse tests reaction time to a virtual fastball traveling at 90mph.

TRY THIS!

Click on the "play ball" button and as soon as you see "swing batter," click on your screen as fast as you can.

This is further enhanced by the addition of interactivity. Here again the background and interests of the designer may be of much greater relevance than anything in the history of animation, which until recently was a linear and passive form. Some interactive elements on an animated Web page allow the user to perform a visual dance on the screen or compose a personal animation. Some are reminiscent of games or puzzles, while some reflect complex three-dimensional structures. Many, of course, are functional elements like rollover buttons, which have no roots in the history of animation. Long before the Internet was even dreamed of, the Science Museum in London used to feature a famous push-button gallery in the basement. Eager children—and adults—would push clunky buttons on large machines reminiscent of early Science Fiction scenarios—and things would happen. Now, more than ever, we are pushing buttons to make things happen. The only difference is that now the buttons, and most of the things happening, are "virtual."

ANIMATION'S LEGACY

14

There can be few Web designers who have not been exposed to a substantial body of traditional animation work in entertainment and advertising. We may not be consciously aware of these influences, but because they often start in early childhood they are remarkably powerful. They are part of the cultural baggage that we continue to carry around with us—for better or worse. And it is inevitable that its influence will creep into our own work—indeed, it is more or less impossible to keep it out. On the positive side, most designers are already in a position to draw on or scavenge a range of features and inspiration from a hundred years of animation history—a solid foundation on which to build.

After a century of investigation, there are few problems connected with sequencing images, or creating and controlling movement within a frame, that have not been gone into. But there are new challenges in Web animation, especially in the realm of interactivity—for example, how to animate the states of a rollover button, or design an animated menu—that differ from the challenges faced by traditional animators and open the way for completely new solutions. There are also new constraints, such as the need to produce small files for download over limited bandwidth. But it remains the case that a great deal of animation on the Web is closely tied to its predigital forebear, and the tasks are much the same as they have always been in animation.

Very often, traditional animation has sought to re-create movements observed in the natural world, even though these may be applied to fictional or fantastic characters and settings. The heritage of character animation and cartoons can be seen in many banner advertisements on Web pages. Few could hope to match

2
A banner ad for TSP uses traditional character animation in a 9-frame animated GIF. The text on white background remains still, accentuating the animation on the left.

1
J. Stuart Blackton's "Humorous Phases of Funny Faces" was made by Vitagraph in 1906. After a century of animation, how much has changed?

A Grand Day Out

Year: 1989
Running Time: 23 minutes
Gauge: 35 mm
Ratio: 1:133
Sound: Mono

Cracking Toast

Wallace and his sophisticated dog Gromit have to decide where to go for their annual picnic. With a home-made rocket and large appetite they head for the moon in search of cheese. Their moon-tasting arouses the anger of the moons resident mechanical caretaker. In the conflict that ensues the earthlings unwittingly help the robot to fulfil its dreams.

See the official Wallace & Gromit site...

3

15

the memorable characterization of Aardman Animations, but many designers carry Wallace and Gromit among their cultural baggage, and traces of these and many other famous animated characters find their way into Web work. From Mickey Mouse through the Pink Panther to the Simpsons and beyond, a host of animated characters provides a source of inspiration.

The influence of predigital animation is not limited to cartoons and character animation. Since the early 20th century, artists have experimented with abstract and experimental animation. Among the techniques that these artists practiced, Oskar Fischinger used real paint on layers of glass in order to build up a sequence of evolving, swirling shapes. Norman MacLaren scratched lines and drew pictures—and sound (!)—directly onto real film stock, and Len Lye stenciled abstract designs onto discarded documentary film footage. Now we often use digital tools to create similar effects—but, although the means have changed, the underlying vision and quest remain. The Web has provided new forums for abstract animation, and many highly thought of designers are experimenting with this form. This exploration feeds back into the design of commercial Web sites and enriches Web animation as a whole.

3
Aardman Animation's famous characters, Wallace and Gromit, were dreamed up by Nick Park while he was at the National Film and Television School (London) in the 1980s. Now Aardman are one of the leading model-animation studios.

4
At www.wmteam.de everything that happens on the site is presented in the form of witty cartoon animation—but this has been used wholly in the service of providing information about the company. The result is charming—and effective.

4

FUNCTION DEFINES FORM

In the predigital history of animation, the question of function in a literal sense did not arise. Animation had a function to entertain, to inform, to draw attention to a product, and so on. But it was never called on to be involved in any action or interaction—so animation designers did not need to give thought to the many difficulties posed by expressing practical functions in a suitably clear form.

For many years before the Internet became a household facility, designers, computer scientists, and experts in human–computer interaction spent much time trying to come up with user-friendly and effective user interfaces. By the time they began designing Web browsers and Web site-authoring tools, conventions for many basic interactions with computer applications had already been established. The scroll bars on the sides of windows, menus that pop up (or down) when selected by mouse, and drag and drop, all preceded mass access to the Internet.

Because it is generally considered poor design practice to confuse the user, the functional animated features that we find on Web pages may derive from earlier design solutions. Thus a Web site will display a menu as a list, close to one side of the window and items on that list will exhibit some obvious change when the mouse rolls over them. If the list is long there will be a recognizable scroll bar to reach the unseen parts, and so

❙ www.petergabriel. com uses a family of similar navigation elements throughout the site. Coded by color, these small abstract rollover buttons—circles on this page—provide a constant set of links. This home page also features a rollover list menu, and a pop-up in the bottom right-hand corner.

on. For most commercial sites the aim is to make using the site as easy and obvious to the user as possible. On a number of sites, the scope for unusual animation of the basic functional elements is limited, and good design consists of producing animation that serves its purpose quickly and effectively. In fact, the relation between many of these functions and their form is a purely arbitrary one, which has been established by widespread adoption. Plus, the designer often has to work with iconic conventions as well, such as the use of a symbol representing a small house to indicate a link to the home page, or an envelope to indicate contact details.

The Web animator has to keep to a set of rules for the functional elements on mainstream sites, and the more functional the site itself is intended to be, the

2

This original interface at www.jpgaultier.fr provides the user with a unique menu in the form of colored bonbons.

As the cursor rolls over each one they swivel and the menu item appears as text, but if the mouse is not used there is no

clue to the site's contents. Linked pairs of bonbons express linked navigation to alternate French and English pages.

stricter the rules become. In e-commerce, for example, it is necessary to get the customer to the checkout with a laden virtual shopping basket as simply as possible. And on Web banking sites it is considered undesirable to have any elements detract from either the serious image of the bank, or the business of managing personal finances.

Where a Web site acts as a showcase for a company, particularly if the company has a bold image, a little more license is available, and if the company is itself part of the design world it may adopt more flamboyant functional elements, such as the bonbons that provide the navigational facilities on the home page of Jean-Paul Gaultier's site. Indeed, designers' own sites, experimental art sites, and online games are at liberty to explore the possibilities for the animation of functional elements as far as they can. In these cases, it can take a while just to discover how to use the site, but this in itself raises interesting questions about interface design, and helps advance our thinking on a topic that is too often given no thought.

3

A straightforward vertical menu of gray buttons, toned in with the page at www.dlxdeluxe.com, reveals tiny surprise Flash animations upon rollover, providing pinpoints of movement and color on an otherwise static page. Transparent functionality is thus combined with classy design and a clever use of animation.

LOOK HERE!

One of the most common uses of animation on Web sites is to say "Look here!". Because we are highly sensitive to movement, the fact that something is moving is usually sufficient to attract notice and animation is the perfect tool for doing this—providing that it can be made to stand out from the rest of the page. Whatever the reason for grabbing attention, animation is being used because of the very fact that it moves. However, it is not sufficient just to catch someone's eye; the viewer's attention must be held long enough for the message to get across. And the length of time that that will take is dependent on the complexity of the message. A warning triangle blinking on and off, or the word "NEW," for example, conveys a simple message quickly. But it is not enough that the viewer simply sees the sign flashing; their attention must be drawn to whatever it is that is new or alarming. The animated sign is only a pointer.

Regardless of why animation is being used to grab attention, it nevertheless requires a suitable environment to do so effectively. If there are many moving elements on a Web page, no single one is likely to stand out. Generally speaking, a contrast is required. Then, if an animated element is competing for attention with a still one, the animation should always win, because movement attracts the eye whether we wish it to or not. Attention-grabbing animation can be a powerful tool, but it has already fallen into disrepute in the context of Web sites, and to be effective it needs to be handled with care. Sites with many advertisements playing all at once are confusing and irritating; a row of constantly animated buttons is visually disorienting; a blinking button or sign quickly gets on the nerves and so on. And badly executed animation is annoying, no matter what its purpose. The more important it is to draw attention to a web page, the better planned the animation should be.

On the site www.bbc.co.uk/weather, a simple animated GIF of a warning triangle flashes from white to red at the top of the page. On a still page this acts as an attention-grabbing link to details of severe weather warnings.

2
Macromedia are well known for carrying public service banner ads on their Web sites. In this case the contrast between the design of the page and the ad itself works in a positive way to draw attention to a charitable message on a commercial site.

19

The most frequent use of attention-grabbing animation is for advertisements, and these pose a number of special problems. For an advertisement to be effective it is vital for the attention to be held long enough to understand what is being advertised. Many viewers may not want to see the advertisement at all—that is not why they came to the Web page. So there are additional hurdles to overcome, and poor animation can easily lose the attention the moment after it has been grabbed. Good or unusual animation, on the other hand, may hold the attention of the viewer even if they have no interest in the product or service being advertised.

What an advertiser must usually persuade the viewer to do is to "click-through"—to click on the advertisement itself in order to follow a link to the advertiser's own site. This is necessary because the advertiser is a paying guest on somebody else's Web page. Not only does this put the advertiser at an immediate practical disadvantage, because the viewer is not actually at their product's site, it creates other difficulties too. As third parties insert the advertisements by arrangement with the host site, they are designed without reference to the

design of the host page on which they appear. This practice inevitably carries a risk of aesthetic discontinuity between the third-party element and other material on the page. If both the advertisement and some of the host page are animated, this potential clash is likely to be worse. And in this conflict both sides may lose.

An animated advertisement may appear in many guises, for example, as an inset to one side of the host page, a flashing button link (positioned almost anywhere), or in a new pop-up window of its own. But the most familiar is perhaps the banner ad. All that the designer of the host site can know is that the advertisement will fit a certain space on the page. (There are currently nine recommended sizes for ads, although many more variants are still in use.) In many cases a site will host a range of banner ads for different companies, supplied from a common source like doubleclick.net, and each will be quite different in design from the others. It is only when companies are able to restrict advertising to their own business or group that it is likely that the advertisement will form a well-integrated part of the page as a whole.

IT'S ALIVE!

In the early days of the World Wide Web it was not easy to make graphic elements move around a Web page. This was because the software we use for motion graphics was still undeveloped, and computer processors were much slower and Internet access was over very low bandwidth connections. Animation performance was poor and download times were high. It was not really until the end of the 1990s, with the development of DHTML and Macromedia Flash 3, and then Flash 4, that motion graphics on the Web really came into its own. With recent increases in bandwidth and advances in hardware, we can now expect that animated pages will play well on "standard" machines.

The development of technologies for motion graphics heralded a new form of expression for animation and graphic design. Although TV and the cinema had previously provided a market for some animated graphic design—in the form of advertising, film credits, station idents, and so on—the quantity was small. In addition, graphic designers still confined their attention to static elements, whether for print or the early Web. In the last few years it has become possible to make the individual elements of a designed page—lines, shapes, text, etc.—move without too much technical knowledge on the part of the designer. This is more than just a new arena in which to present motion graphics—it is a completely unprecedented context. The possibilities offered to Web-page elements are different from those offered by film or television, where graphic design is placed in a medium that is both wholly time-based and linear. It is as though printed pages suddenly acquired the potential to come to life.

Because graphic design had previously been focused on print media, it was not easy for designers to transfer their skills to the new, time-based medium. The art of making a visual composition look compelling in a static display is very different from that of making it look compelling throughout a time-based moving presentation. One of the major challenges for this kind of animation derives from the fact that there are few

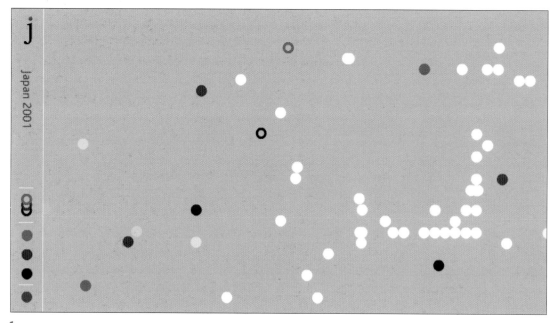

The Japan 2001 Web site at www.nihongocentre.org.uk features sparse motion graphics in Flash, which are both aesthetically pleasing and functionally clear. The colored circles are buttons; the white ones are decoration, in an animation of constant ebb and flow.

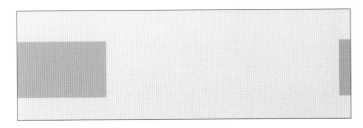

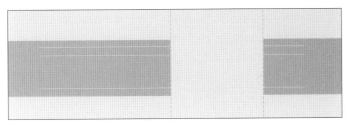

criteria governing what it should look like. In some cases, motion graphics on the Web can borrow from older media like TV advertising or idents, but where it is used to animate the graphic design of the page itself there are no precedents to refer to. And, because it is new, it lacks a set of conventions to adopt or defy.

It is too soon for the merger between animation and graphic design to be complete, but there is some very good work on the World Wide Web. For a while, motion graphics on the Web—especially when it took the form of splash movies requiring lengthy download times—had a bad name. Many users did not want to defer their main mission in visiting sites just in order to see some animated graphics— especially if they were slow and poorly executed. They were in a hurry to find information, do some shopping, or just to get where they were going.

This unfortunately led to something of a backlash, with Flash in particular coming in for some heavy criticism, and companies actually removing motion graphics from their Web sites. But the quality of work has vastly improved over the last couple of years, and the technology is more or less ready to deliver motion graphics properly, providing we are not too ambitious. The challenge now is to persuade companies disillusioned with motion graphics to reinvest in animation, and then to produce animated graphic design that defines the new form.

2

At www.precinct.net, the page for issue 3 opens with a smooth animation. The graphic elements of the page appear to build while we watch, but in reality the method of design for such a page is quite different from the fictional construction process that the Flash movie suggests.

21

ENRICHING EXPERIENCE

Interactivity is acknowledged as a crucial process in education of all kinds, so interactive animation is a key tool for education on the Internet. It is the magic ingredient that can convert something dull and therefore likely to be passed over into something we want to stop and examine. The opportunity to play with objects is hard to resist. Something that moves is more fun than something that's still, and if it responds to our input it is even better.

The Exploratorium in San Francisco has made use of animation on its Web site to present a series of demonstrations of optical illusions that are genuinely astonishing—and surprisingly difficult to get right. The animated interactive exhibits at www.exploratorium.edu/exhibits/ challenge the viewer to apparently simple tasks, like trying to match the sizes of two circles, or the colors of two adjacent areas by means of RGB sliders. The clarity of the animation design, combined with the functionality of the interactive controls, admirably demonstrates the educational point being made while providing a tantalizing and rewarding user experience.

For some educational presentations it is sufficient just to sit, watch, and learn. The time-based nature of animation makes it particularly suitable for conveying the impression of things happening in which one thing follows another. Although we are used to comic-book conventions, and so find it easy to read a static series of images as an unfolding narrative, animation is more effective at conveying developments over time—for

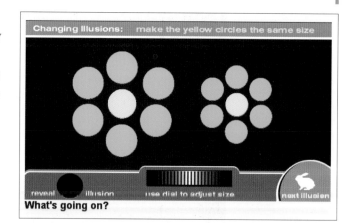

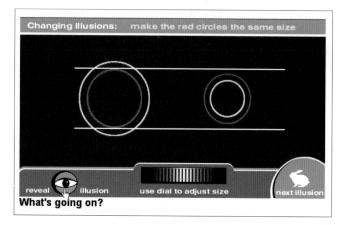

1 | 2
The interactive optical illusion exhibits at the Exploratorium's site encourage users to explore the illusions by means of basic controls such as a shuttle wheel. Deviation from the correct answer is demonstrated by clicking on the reveal button.

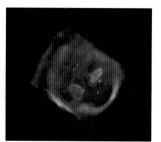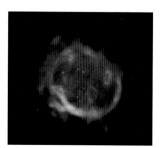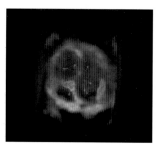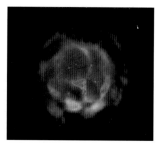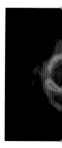

3
Visit NASA's site at spaceflight.nasa.gov and take a virtual tour of parts of the International Space Station. The tour, created in VRML, can also be downloaded to disk for extended study or play.

4
Visualizations may be enticing even when the subject matter is obscure. Chemists at Darmstadt make small MPEG movies of their visualizations available. The one running across the bottom of the page shows the visualization of a 3D data field using 3D texture mapping.

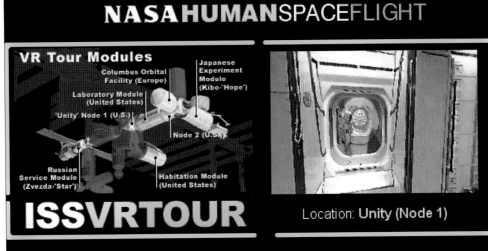

NASAHUMANSPACEFLIGHT

VR Tour Modules

Columbus Orbital Facility (Europe)

Japanese Experiment Module (Kibo-'Hope')

Laboratory Module (United States)

'Unity' Node 1 (U.S.)

Node 2 (U.S.)

Russian Service Module (Zvezda-'Star')

Habitation Module (United States)

ISSVRTOUR

Location: **Unity (Node 1)**

The ISS Joint Airlock, scheduled to arrive on Flight 7A, provides access to the vacuum of space for EVA capability. The Joint Airlock is the prime site for EMU-based EVAs and is capable of supporting Orlan-based EVAs. It is connected to the starboard side of Unity by the Space Station Remote Manipulator System (SSRMS), also known as the Space Station robot arm. The two distinctive components of the Joint Airlock are the Equipment Lock and the Crew Lock.

example, how Captain Cook's route in the *Endeavour* progressed, or how a butterfly emerges from a chrysalis. Such developments may sometimes be displayed as a smooth-playing Flash or Shockwave movie, in which one thing seamlessly follows another, but more basic means may serve as well. A sequence of still images displayed on the same spot like a simple slide show, with an adequate delay between changeovers, may be the ideal way to show how changes occur through time—for example, how weather develops over 24 hours.

In scientific fields visualization techniques have long been used to make the unseeable visible, and to present data in an accessible form. Animation on the Web has extended these principles and made it possible for these same techniques to be employed more generally, and for the results to be available to anyone with a modem. Any data, from official government statistics to the standing wave pattern of an electron, may be portrayed visually, and any scene or object, real or abstract, can be given life through animation on the Web.

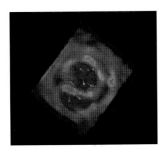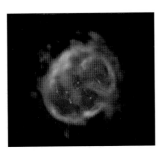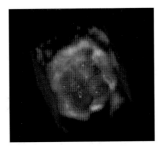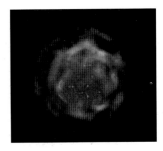

PUSHING THE ENVELOPE

Most forms of entertainment in the real world have found expression on the World Wide Web. In certain areas, notably computer games and online cartoons (called "webisodes"), Web animation is really pushing out the boundaries.

It is reckoned that around two-thirds of Americans now regularly play computer games, many of them online. This is not only entertainment, it is big business, and the customers are notoriously demanding. At all levels—the underlying technologies, the aesthetics of visual design, the challenges of creating convincing movement, interface design, and the design and use of interactive elements—games are pushing the envelope online, just as they have done offline.

Online games developers fall broadly into two camps. On the one hand are the giants. They have the money to invest in the necessary research and development work—and equipment—and for some time have been a major propulsive power behind advances in hardware and software. Sony is one of these giants. They provide a wide range of online games at their Station Web site—from relatively simple puzzles to the 3D, massively multiplayer, fantasy role-playing game

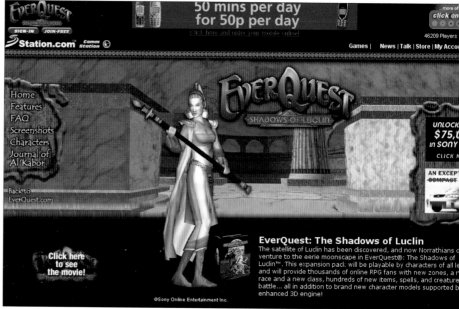

EverQuest: The Shadows of Luclin
The satellite of Luclin has been discovered, and now Norrathians [can] venture to the eerie moonscape in EverQuest®: The Shadows of Luclin™. This expansion pack will be playable by characters of all le[vels] and will provide thousands of online RPG fans with new zones, a [new] race and a new class, hundreds of new items, spells, and creature[s to] battle... all in addition to brand new character models supported b[y an] enhanced 3D engine!

©Sony Online Entertainment Inc.

1
Sony's massively multi-player game EverQuest continues to push the boundaries of online gaming on the technological and business fronts. It has over 400,000 active subscribers, and is in a state of constant ongoing development.

2
Recent animation graduate and Web site designer Marc Jones has adapted free Flash source code to give the classic game, Tetris, a completely new look at www.indigoice.co.uk/ spiltvarnish. It looks different, it plays well, and it's free.

EverQuest. Although first released a couple of years ago, EverQuest, which comprises many worlds, continues to grow and develop, and is a massive project in every sense. Running on around 1,000 servers, each EverQuest world can support up to 3,500 players. For this game alone, Sony uses around 1Gbps of bandwidth at peak times—when there can be up to 96,000 simultaneous players online—and terabytes of disk storage. More importantly, EverQuest is also intensively animated—in real-time 3D. This is a pay-for-play game—naturally, considering what kind of investment is involved—but Sony offer many other smaller games online for free.

At the other end of the spectrum are the little guys—the individuals or small companies who create Internet games just for fun, and who often make them available for free. Although they are inevitably less ambitious, these games developers enjoy a creative freedom similar to that of independent designers working on personal sites, and so it is often among these little games that gems of quirky and original animation ideas are found. Sometimes they involve creative programming, which pushes the boundaries on that plane too.

Games are not the only form of entertainment on the Web, however. Pleasurable relaxation may no doubt be derived from Web sites of various kinds, but from an animator's point of view there is a type of Web entertainment of particular relevance—animation itself. There are now many sites devoted purely to the online presentation of animation of all kinds, from cutting edge abstract experimental work that wins awards at film festivals, to showcases for recent graduates, to webisodes—cartoons created specially for the Web shown in weekly or other regular episodes. While this area may not seem to present demands comparable to those of games design, there are a surprising number of difficulties in getting any sustained piece of animation to play satisfactorily over the Internet, and therefore as many challenges for the designers who are called upon to create effective webisodes and other online animation for entertainment as those who design for games.

3

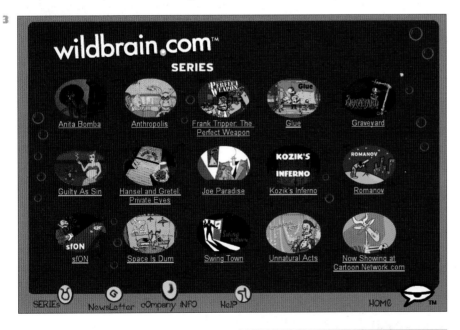

3 | 4
www.wildbrain.com is the Internet animation site of one of the biggest US animation studios. It presents classic cartoon skills in the digital environment, with webisodes aimed at a teen and adult audience. Swingtown features stylish graphics in a cult/ noir setting.

4

THE OUTER LIMITS

The World Wide Web has so far provided an unprecedented opportunity for anyone wishing to exhibit their work. Providing they have access to a means of digital production, and require no more Web facilities than the average ISP will provide for free, any artist or designer can create an electronic masterpiece and show it, at no cost, to the world at large. With funding, established artists and designers can produce and run Web sites that challenge and redefine the nature and uses of animation. And that is exactly what many of them are doing. For anyone interested in Web animation it is among these sites—which feature personal work and ongoing projects—that the most exciting and most advanced use of the medium is found.

The technologies that support this work are still young and in a state of flux. Each year, enhanced versions of existing software are released. Sometimes—in the case of the revision of Flash ActionScript, for example— these changes inspire a whole new round of experimentation. Occasionally, completely new products emerge that can alter both what we can do, and how we can do it. And continuing advances in hardware mean that animation can play faster, and interactive features respond more quickly. There is a constant drive forward, which is often exploited by talented people who have nothing to lose—either because they are already so well established that experimentation is expected, or because they are so little known that they can only gain by exposing their work.

There is always an element of risk involved in working in the avant-garde. Many of the great artists of the past were faced with ridicule, not to mention poverty, as a result of experiments that in retrospect we

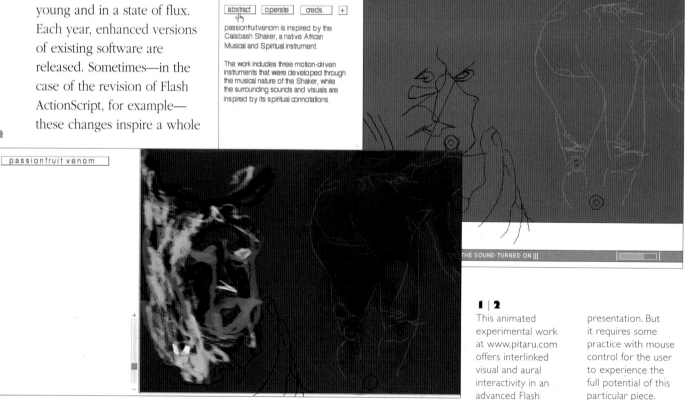

passionfruit venom

abstract | operate | creds. | +

passionfruitvenom is inspired by the Calabash Shaker, a native African Musical and Spiritual instrument.

The work includes three motion-driven instruments that were developed through the musical nature of the Shaker, while the surrounding sounds and visuals are inspired by its spiritual connotations.

passionfruit venom

THE SOUND TURNED ON]]]

1 | 2
This animated experimental work at www.pitaru.com offers interlinked visual and aural interactivity in an advanced Flash presentation. But it requires some practice with mouse control for the user to experience the full potential of this particular piece.

3

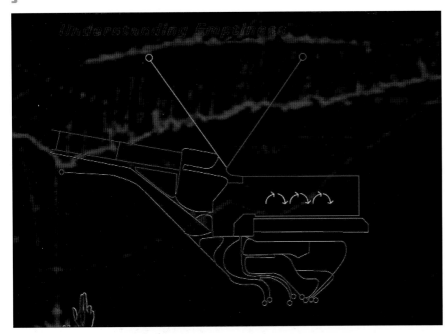

3 | 4

Empty Velocity by
Angie Eng is part of
www.turbulence.org's
program of
commissioning and
exhibiting online art.
Although made in
1999 with DHTML it
remains highly
effective within the
experimental
context. Here "you
will learn to travel
in time and space
in stillness."

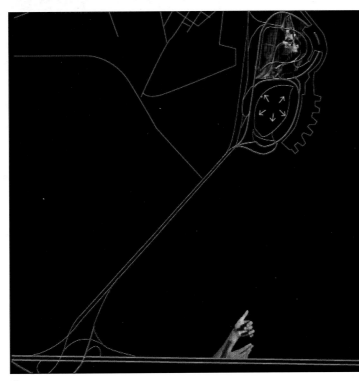

4

see as great advances in the history of art. Fortunately for experimental Web animators, the enormous reach of the Web means that there is almost certainly somebody out there who is capable of appreciating our work right now. More often than not there are many other people involved in similar areas, or interested in experimental work generally, which means that support networks can develop.

Artists working at the cutting edge have often formed supportive groups, or at least loose associations, in order to exchange ideas. Now it is possible to network across the world with people we have never met but who share our interests, appreciate our work, and provide sources of inspiration that we can develop and then feed back. This interconnectivity is a fertile breeding ground for new ideas. In the early 20th century the development of abstraction by Picasso and other artists altered the nature of all the graphic arts. In the same way, the ideas and techniques worked out through experimentation with Web animation will form the basis of advances in more conventional design and practice in years to come.

THE FOURTH DIMENSION

One vital element sets animation apart from the other graphic elements on a Web page: not that it involves the illusion of movement within a space, but that it is concerned entirely with changes over time.

Animation is a time-based medium—and yet even in this context it is unique, because it is the only one of the time-based media that is created from static elements. Although video and film record a series of still images to be played back quickly, they nevertheless attempt to make and present a convincing record of actual movement. Sound is different: it is a continuous phenomenon, only perceptible because we are adapted to detect the movements in the air that it creates, and to interpret them as sound. For the purposes of recording and playback it may be broken down into discrete samples, but it requires a huge number of such samples per second to create a convincing impression. And when they are played back the way in which it works—the movement of the air—remains the same. Sound cannot exist except as a continuous event through time.

So animation forms a unique bridge between the timeless and the timed. Made up of elements which in themselves have no relation to or dependence on time (they are just still graphics), it comes into existence only when these are presented in a sequence through time. It is said of traditional animation that it does not matter what each drawing is like, it is what happens between

them that counts. This is an exaggeration, of course, but it points to a fundamental truth: it is the relation between each frame or state of an animation that makes it good or bad.

When animation reached the World Wide Web strange things started to happen. Before the use of digital media traditional animation was linear. It proceeded in one direction along a predetermined path. It had a beginning, middle, and an end. But on the Web we are no longer dealing with a linear environment. And in many cases the way in which things will proceed cannot be predetermined by their creators. Even a straightforward animated GIF may never get a chance to finish, or may play many times in a row, depending on what the viewer of the page is up to. The designer has no idea of the order in which a user will rollover a set of menu buttons on a page—no foreknowledge of the order of play. Animation is still time-based, but in this nonlinear, nondeterministic environment, time is not as it used to be.

However, it is still possible to control things up to a point. We can foresee the order of playback within restricted contexts. A rollover will have two or more states, and we know which one can follow which. An animated GIF may be stopped in midplay, but the order of the frames cannot be changed. A Flash or Shockwave presentation will proceed in the way the designer

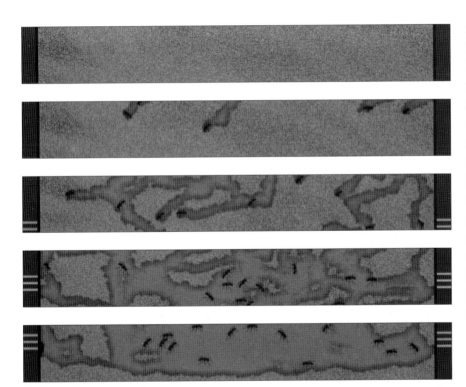

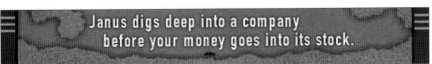

Janus digs deep into a company
before your money goes into its stock.

J A N U S | Get there.

Janus Distributors, Inc.

intended while the page works. Interaction will only be within the limits that the designer has set. So the necessity to design coherent sequences remains, although this operates in an unpredictable context. And the fact that the environment is more complex that the old linear forms makes it more necessary to understand and plan how each sequence will work. On the Web, animation is not just concerned with creating an illusion of movement, but with sequencing images in time. How those images relate to one another is fundamental.

1
Animators plan how to sequence images in time through the use of storyboards and animatics. Aardman shows how this works in a slide show animatic shown at www.aardman.com /wallaceandgromit /workshop.

2
In Freestyle Interactive's Ant Farm banner ad for Janus, the ants tunnel through the ground. Careful sequencing is required to convey quite a complex visual message in the restricted time and space of a banner ad.

FIGURES OF MOTION

The illusion of motion is created in moving pictures because of a phenomenon called persistence of vision. This means that if we are shown a sequence of static images at sufficient speed, we perceive the changes between them as motion. To produce an impression of realistic motion, the pictures have to play at a rate of 24 frames per second (24 fps) or faster, but often a speed of 12 fps, or less, is adequate for animation. This is just as true for animation on the Web. Therefore the primary challenge for any Web designer creating moving animation is to produce the right amount of change between each frame. This is not a fixed measure, but a quantity that will vary according to the artwork and design. However, it can be broadly specified as the amount of change that will result in an illusion of motion being perceived when the animation is played back at the specified frame rate. Determining and creating this is the key skill in animation of motion.

Len Lye, a New Zealand-born artist who worked in many artforms during his lifetime, made a few short films that are among the classics of abstract and experimental animation. On the official, www.govettb.org.nz/lenlye, he is quoted as saying:

All of a sudden it hit me—if there was such a thing as composing music, there could be such a thing as composing motion. After all, there are melodic figures, why can't there be figures of motion?

Not all designers of Web animation will have heard of Len Lye, but some continue in his footsteps, whether they are aware of it or not. And for all animators who wish to create an illusion of movement—especially those working with abstract graphic elements, or a combination of abstraction and representation—his insight will ring true.

A short clip from Len Lye's experimental animated film Free Radicals is shown as an embedded QuickTime movie in a drive-in movie setting at media2.cs.berkeley.edu /webvideo/people/ sandy/lenlye.html.

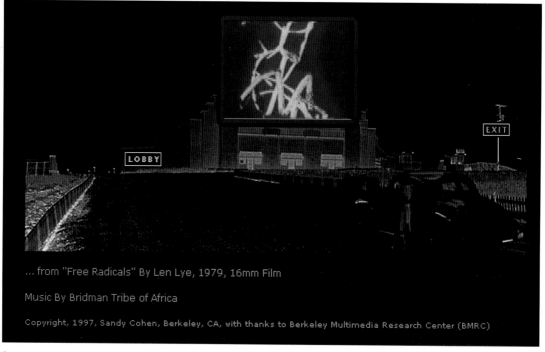

... from "Free Radicals" By Len Lye, 1979, 16mm Film

Music By Bridman Tribe of Africa

Copyright, 1997, Sandy Cohen, Berkeley, CA, with thanks to Berkeley Multimedia Research Center (BMRC)

What distinguishes successful abstract animation and motion graphics is often not the design of the graphic elements themselves but the choreography of the piece as a whole. Not only must the illusion of motion be appropriate for the pace and flow of every individual element, but each one must interact with the rest to create a complete composition. If an animation does not involve characters, recognizable objects, scenes, or textual elements, then it consists only of graphic marks, abstract 3D objects, and movement. When creating abstract animation, therefore, the designer must focus on rhythm, pacing, the grouping of elements, use of the window as a stage, and so on. In elaborate animations it may be necessary to choreograph different sets of movements, rhythms, and groupings—perhaps even a number of separate animations or windows—in such a way that they all work together.

Abstraction helps to clarify many of the problems that occur in all animations of motion, but animation that involves characters or representational elements brings additional difficulties. Animators are often advised to imagine themselves inside the character—to feel the movement from within. That is all very well if the animated element represents a living creature, but it's not so easy if it is a table. The animation of a real or imagined creature can be partly drawn from life; the animation of objects must be wholly imagined. With this kind of animation, there are two practical choices. Either the object is given something of the characteristic movements of a living creature—or it must be choreographed as though it were an abstract element, so that it works as part of a visually coherent whole.

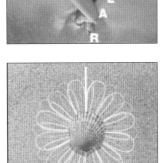

2

The motion graphics in the Natural Life window from issue 3 at www.precinct.net have been coordinated and paced very carefully so that the sum of the individual parts forms a pleasing choreographed whole.

WHERE NEXT?

Bits and Pieces

Web animation has come a long way during its short existence, but we are still just at the beginning of the road. Because so much depends on technological advances, it is not easy to look very far ahead. It is vital, then, that Web animators remain ready to take on new challenges and grasp new opportunities.

It is a very exciting time for anyone working in this area—but frustrating too. Very often ideas outstrip the ability of technology to deliver: bandwidth is too narrow; computer processors are too slow; software is buggy or does not do what we want. In order to create successful work now, we have to study and understand these limitations and learn how to work within them. On the Internet a clever idea is not enough. It has to work—and it has to work not only on the superfast machine we have created it on, but also the other machines out there in the world, which are connected to the Internet at different speeds and use different Web browsers.

Nothing is more irritating to the user—or even to the animator or designer who understands the problems—than to find that what they want to look at on the Web does not work. It makes no difference to the user why it fails. If it fails, that is the end of the story. We have to accept that it is probably impossible to please all of the people—or all of the browsers—all of the time. There are just too many variables. But we should at least make our best efforts to please most of them most of the time. And that means getting to grips with the technologies.

In Web animation, to a greater extent than in layout, or in the design of still graphics and textual elements, there are many brick walls we run up against, because we are frequently asking more of the technologies involved. However, constraints can have a positive influence on design, while complete freedom can make work—and life—much more difficult. To avoid unnecessary grief when designing animation for the Web, it is advisable to be adequately briefed on the nature of the constraints and limitations—and on what will and will not work within them.

In one sense it is unfortunate that things keep changing. It means that we have to keep up, expanding last year's ideas to fit the larger size of this year's technology. But a positive attitude will usually lead to the most creative results, and there are at least two ways to approach this difficulty successfully. For those who welcome new challenges and can keep pace with technology, the fast rate of change acts as a positive stimulus. And for those who prefer to focus on one challenge, and take time to perfect their response, the changes simply make things work better.

At one time the animated GIF was the only real viable option for playing a rapid sequence of images on a Web page. While we now have other more

1

Daniel Brown's collection of advanced Shockwave "Bits and Pieces," exhibited at www.noodlebox.com, features some beautiful images, remarkable animation, and impressive interactivity.

2

All the animals at www.bemboszoo.com are created entirely with elements from the font. Flash makes it happen, but it is the understated simplicity of both the idea and its execution that makes this site outstanding.

2

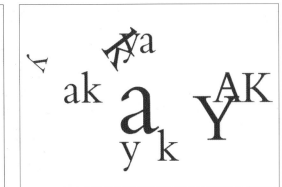

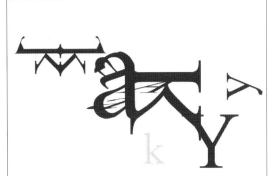

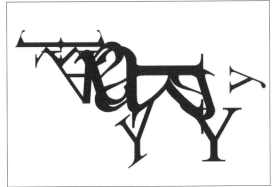

33

sophisticated choices, such as Flash and Shockwave, the humble animated GIF is still with us, and because of technological advances it has not been totally surpassed—it can now be made larger and play faster than ever before. It is very rarely the case that if something works well on poor technology it will work less well when the technology is improved. So our aim as animation artists need only be to make as good work under the current technological conditions as we can. If we can achieve this, progress will take care of itself.

INTERNET ACCESS AND BANDWIDTH

Web animation appears only on the Internet. Therefore the constraints that limit what we can achieve relate mainly to Internet performance and user access. There is no way the designer can know what kind of access to their work each individual viewer has.

In the last few years, there have been substantial changes in telecommunications infrastructures, so that there are now many possible Internet connection speeds. The first consideration, therefore, is bandwidth—the rate of data transfer available to users. This is determined by the kind of telecommunications service used, together with the type of hardware or modem used. A 56 kbps (V90 standard) modem on an ordinary telephone line is still the standard connection for domestic consumers. In fact, many may still be using 28.8 kbps modems, which are

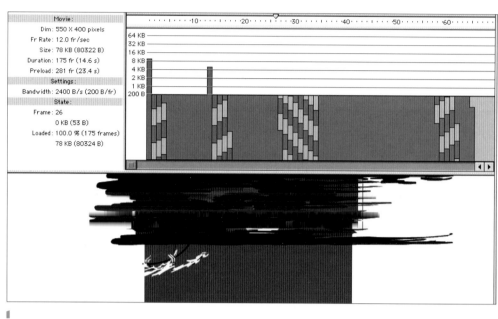

1

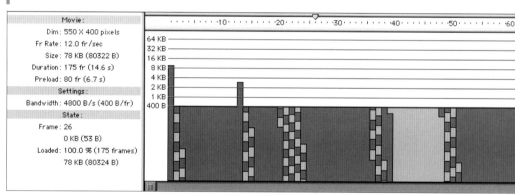

2

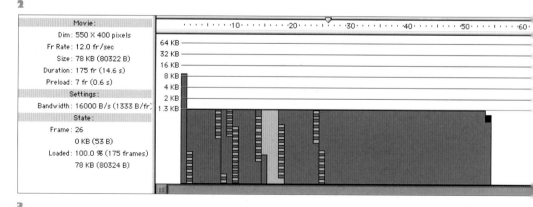

3

36

much slower; in less technologically advanced parts of the world users are likely to have even lower bandwidth capabilities. And if these speeds sound low, the actual rate of data transfer is worse: a 56 kbps modem will provide a rate of only 38 to 48 kbps.

Among more affluent users, and in urban areas, pure digital connections are increasingly common. A single channel ISDN line guarantees a rate of 64 kbps, which can be doubled up to 128 kbps. The newest digital technologies send digital data down the voice bandwidth. ADSL (asymmetric digital subscriber line) provides up to 1 Mbps (mega bit per second) from server to client (less in the other direction), and cable modems provide the same. However, with a cable connection this is shared by the users on the same line, so bandwidth may be reduced, and it suffers even further from high demand. Even though these digital connections sound very fast, it is sobering to reflect that a 2x CD-ROM plays at 2.4 Mbps, and a 12x CD-ROM will give a data transfer rate two hundred and sixty times as fast as a normal domestic modem.

1 | 2 | 3

The bandwidth profiler in Flash allows us to check how movies play over different connection speeds. These three images show how a multilayered animation will stream over 28.8 kbps, 56 kbps, and dual ISDN connections (specified in the histogram in bytes per second). The movie is straightforward, but only ISDN is fast enough for streaming.

What does all this mean in practice? It is clear that there is a huge difference in access speeds for users, and many people are using low-bandwidth connections, so it is prudent to ensure that work performs adequately at low speeds. And compared with anything that happens inside a computer, or in transfer from a typical CD-ROM, those speeds are excruciatingly slow. For animation, the primary concern is download time. Although streaming technology is supposed to make it possible to play moving pictures live across the Internet, it cannot deliver the data fast enough for continuous playback on low bandwidths. The options are to partly download and then attempt streaming, or to fully download before playback starts. The second option is more appropriate, and almost always more reliable.

Over a slow connection the user will even have to wait for an animated GIF to arrive; a Flash movie, Shockwave presentation or anything involving virtual reality will take much longer. A typical 300 kb Flash movie for a corporate site takes around a minute to download via a 56 kbps modem, and very often there is nothing else happening during that time. A minute is a long time for someone to twiddle their thumbs. And it should not be forgotten that in many parts of the world users are paying by the minute for their Internet connections, and do not enjoy the unmetered access pioneered in the US.

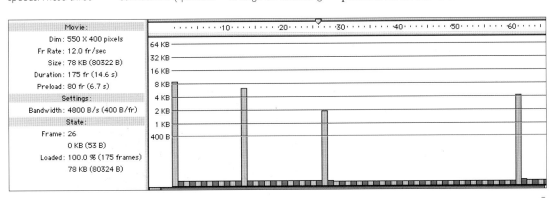

Movie:
Dim: 550 X 400 pixels
Fr Rate: 12.0 fr/sec
Size: 78 KB (80322 B)
Duration: 175 fr (14.6 s)
Preload: 80 fr (6.7 s)
Settings:
Bandwidth: 4800 B/s (400 B/fr)
State:
Frame: 26
0 KB (53 B)
Loaded: 100.0 % (175 frames)
78 KB (80324 B)

4
Another option shows the size of each frame in an animation relative to a specified bandwidth. This helps identify the point at which a pre-loading sequence can stop and move on to the main movie.

4

37

UNPREDICTABLE ELEMENTS

Unpredictable elements at the user's end can be responsible for many disasters, from visual distortion of a Web page to the failure of animation playback or interactive functionality.

The biggest troublemakers are the Web browsers themselves. There are several browsers available, but Netscape Navigator and Microsoft Internet Explorer are the most widely used. One might think that Web browsers would be required to conform to a world-wide standard. Not so. The World Wide Web Consortium can only make recommendations, and until recently Microsoft and Netscape have neglected these in their competition to provide new features. Even within the same developer there is no consistency. Version 5 of Explorer for the Mac conforms to the standards, but the same version for Windows does not.

If Web site designers stick to basic HTML there should not be many problems with the browsers; the trouble starts when dynamic HTML is used. (DHTML comprises HTML plus JavaScript plus CSS.) In particular, Navigator and Explorer have differences in the way they refer to document elements in JavaScript, which means that separate code has to be written for the same page to operate under the different browsers. And to make matters worse, different previously released versions of these browsers which are inconsistent with one another are still in use. Web-authoring applications such as Adobe GoLive or Macromedia Dreamweaver help by providing tools for checking compatibility of pages with different browser options, but this is not foolproof. Few Web users have not come across JavaScript and other errors when accessing Web sites.

The headaches of trying to make Web work safe on all browsers can be avoided by using technologies that depend upon plug-ins. These extend the capabilities of the browser and provide a more dependable environment for specific kinds of files. Flash,

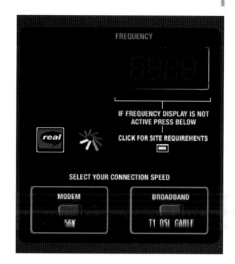

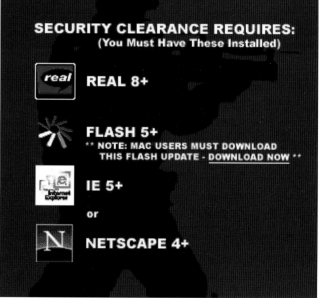

1 | 2
At www.rsub.com there is no uncertainty about what is required from the user.

3
Flash and Shockwave are dependable—but the no-plug-in icon is not a welcome sight for users hoping to see an exciting piece of interactive animation.

38

Shockwave, QuickTime, Windows Media, and various other formats, including several proprietary virtual reality formats, all require plug-ins in the user's browser in order for anything made with these to work. Plug-ins are not trouble-free, but they are relatively foolproof compared with the use of DHTML.

We cannot know what size screen and what resolution a viewer will be using—and all of a page that fits a large screen at high resolution will not be seen on a smaller screen, or at a lower resolution. There is a wide range of monitors on the market, and no one standard resolution. So designers working on large

studio screens—say 19 inches or bigger—and at relatively high resolutions, need to remember that few consumers will have this kind of equipment. The largest commonly used domestic monitors have 17-inch screens, and resolution is unlikely to be set higher than 1024 x 768 pixels. Many will be using lower resolutions and smaller screens; the iMac, for example, has only a 15-inch screen, and although it will display at 1024 x 768, many users prefer 800 x 600. To avoid uncertainty about what the user will see, the safest course to ensure that all the work is seen on the screen is to use JavaScript to spawn a new window of an appropriate fixed size.

39

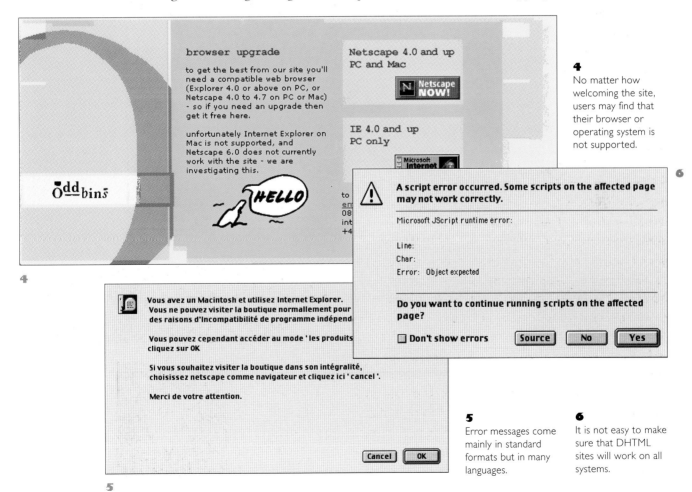

4
No matter how welcoming the site, users may find that their browser or operating system is not supported.

4

5

5
Error messages come mainly in standard formats but in many languages.

6
It is not easy to make sure that DHTML sites will work on all systems.

COLOR: BETTER SAFE THAN SORRY

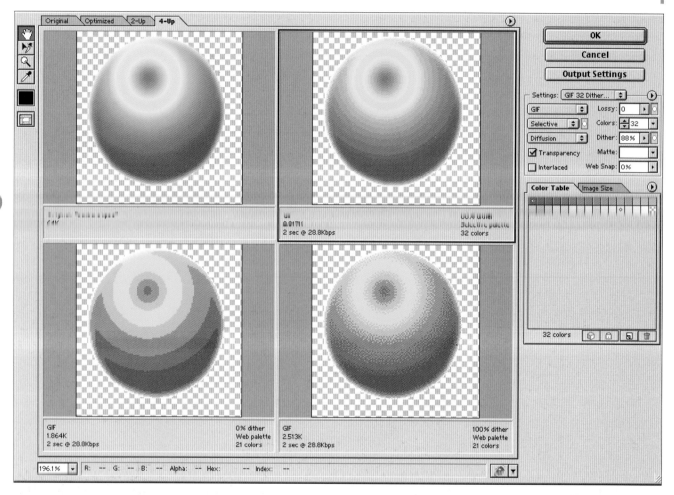

There are two reasons why the colors we use in Web design may not appear as we intended on the viewer's screen, and both arise from the hardware and software that the viewer is using.

First, different computer systems have different methods of mapping stored color values to the displayed color values on a monitor. Windows will give a much darker display of the same image than will be seen with Mac settings. On some systems it is possible for the user to adjust display settings, including colors. Second the number of different colors a system can

display—the color depth—will vary. Contemporary computing equipment is often capable of displaying millions of colors (except at very high resolutions). For every pixel in an image it uses 8 bits for each of the three color channels: red, green, and blue. This is therefore referred to as 24-bit color, and it allows for millions of permutations of color mixes. However, until recently computers used 15- or 16-bit color (thousands of colors) and PCs intended for business used 8-bit color. Eight bits may not sound much less than 24 bits, but in fact the difference is enormous. An 8-bit color depth gives a maximum of 256 different colors—a severe limitation for designers—while 24-bit color is capable of producing any color that could be distinguished on a computer screen.

On an 8-bit color PC, which can use a total of just 256 colors, the Windows colormap defines 232 colors, of which 16 are the original VGA color palette used by MS-DOS, and the other 216 are fixed. This leaves just 24 colors that may be undefined and so customized. Although many systems are capable of displaying a greater range of colors, the 216 fixed colors from the Windows colormap have become the standard Web-safe palette. If designers use only these colors, any system should be able to display them.

In a world with millions of colors, this seems an unreasonable limitation, and many designers ignore it. However, for Web animation it is important. Animated GIFs were conceived before modern 24-bit color systems, and are restricted to a maximum of 256 colors. Fortunately, however, they implement a compromise: rather than using the Web-safe palette, we can use a 256-color custom palette derived from the artwork itself. This allows for more subtle colors: 256 shades chosen from a restricted palette can give a good result for any image. But viewers without adequate systems will not be able to see our custom colors—either the image will be displayed highly posterized, or it will be dithered (*see* Glossary).

41

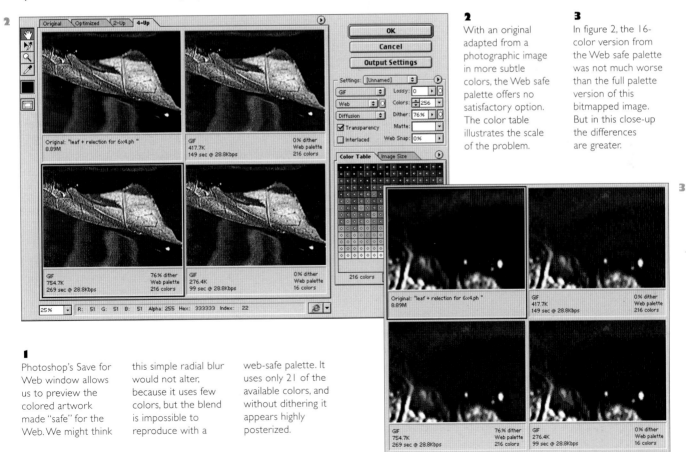

2

2
With an original adapted from a photographic image in more subtle colors, the Web safe palette offers no satisfactory option. The color table illustrates the scale of the problem.

3
In figure 2, the 16-color version from the Web safe palette was not much worse than the full palette version of this bitmapped image. But in this close-up the differences are greater.

3

1
Photoshop's Save for Web window allows us to preview the colored artwork made "safe" for the Web. We might think this simple radial blur would not alter, because it uses few colors, but the blend is impossible to reproduce with a web-safe palette. It uses only 21 of the available colors, and without dithering it appears highly posterized.

IF THE CAP FITS

There is more than one way to design and deliver most kinds of Web animation. So there is no straightforward answer to the question: "What is the right tool for this job?" The choice of technology will depend on the software and expertise available to the designer, or on personal preference. It is just not possible to say "Do this kind of animation in this way, and that kind in that way."

Consider the case of a rollover button, for example. In the early days of the Web the separate states of the button would have been designed in a still-image application, or a 3D program, and the function controlled by JavaScript. There is nothing wrong with this: it still works the

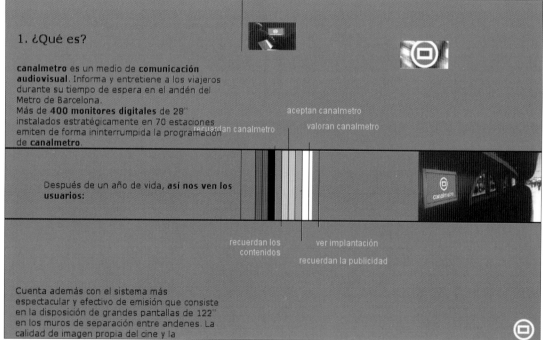

1
The home page at www.plaino.com is static apart from some in-place and remote rollovers. It could have been made with DHTML, but is a Flash site.

2
www.canalmetro.net has motion graphics, and windows that appear and disappear in different places. It might look like Flash, but it's all DHTML.

same way that it ever did. But now we have more choice. Flash, in particular, has become an attractive alternative for designing and implementing these Web animation elements, as well as complex movies and interactivity. Many sites now feature Flash rollovers and menu bars; they work well and are easy to create for designers who are familiar with Flash but not confident with DHTML.

If we do still want to use JavaScript to do this kind of animation work, it is no longer necessary to write the code by hand or to know how it works. Contemporary applications streamline the whole process, from the design of the rollover button to its implementation within a Web page. Adobe ImageReady, for example, facilitates the creation of rollovers, including the animated states, and works with GoLive to make the rollovers active within a Web page, without the designer having to grapple personally with HTML and JavaScript.

If we want to play a fully animated sequence on a Web page, there is again a choice of methods. The animated GIF works better than it has ever done and avoids the use of plug-ins or other unpredictable elements at the user's end. However, to use these we must accept a limited color palette, and keep the animation short and small. Flash, on the other hand, although primarily a vector graphics application, actually handles bitmaps quite well, and so could be used to play the same material as an animated GIF.

For sophisticated interactivity within Web animation, Flash, or Shockwave are good choices. As the two do not share the same scripting language (alas!), the choice will often depend on the designer's skills. Shockwave handles richer media types, and is free of that Flash "look," which it can be

difficult to avoid in Flash work. And then there is Java. For designers with programming skills (or programmers on hand) Java offers the greatest potential for powerful and original interactivity—with some very efficient means of creating animation—with the advantage that it is the standard language for the World Wide Web and so should run anywhere.

Although some types of animation design will immediately suggest a certain technology, in many cases there is a real choice. And it is worth remembering that the most sophisticated results do not require the most complex means. Conversely, the use of advanced technologies is no guarantee of a good piece of work. You should choose the tool that you are most comfortable with and expresses your creative ideas.

3

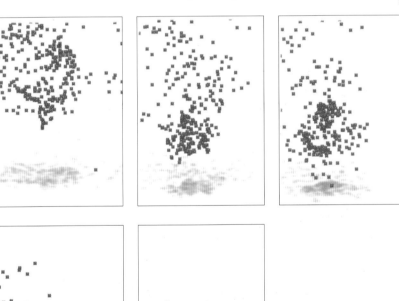

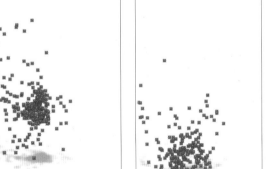

3
This animation by Freestyle Interactive interacts with mouse movement. Something similar to this Java animation may be made in Flash or Shockwave.

THE ANIMATED GIF

The animated GIF is unique among Web image file formats. Created by CompuServe in the late 1980s to facilitate the exchange of graphics between different computer platforms, it was designed from the first to contain several different images within the same file. First defined in 1987 as GIF87a, the specification has only been revised once, two years later. Despite everything that has happened on the World Wide Web since, we are still using GIF89a. However, in this version it is possible to specify a delay time between the display of images—which equates, in animators' terms, to a frame rate. So in 1989 the GIF became capable of playing images as an animation.

Although the animated GIF is a dinosaur now in Web terms, it is still widely used. Its advantages are that it will play on any browser without the need for a plug-in, and it can be easily made by anyone with basic graphics software. There are even freeware and shareware packages available for creating animated GIFs. The animated GIF, then, can be made by anyone, and viewed by everyone. However, it should not be looked down upon. Not only is it the standard format for

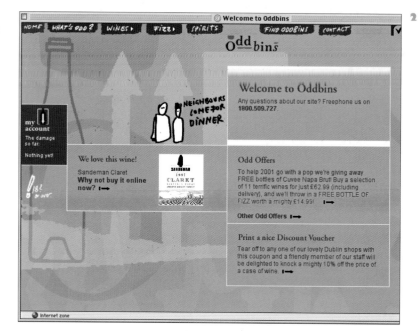

1
The sequence of frames in an animated GIF does not need to convey a smooth transition. This stylish 3–frame button on www.swatch.com exploits the GIF's bitmapped format.

2 | 3
Bold artwork can be effective in a small animated GIF, even on a large page. The animated GIFs at www.oddbins. com/ireland are the only moving elements on the page and stand out well.

3

44

  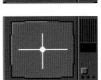 

4

Animated GIFs can convey a message using few colors. "TV's bad for you" by Marc Wielogroch was made with Alan Watts' 16-color program and is part of the Internet Movie Machine at www.16color.com.

5

Animated GIFs can imitate effects like film transitions despite their limitations. This animated button at everquest.station.sony. com/luclin uses dissolves with a limited range of colors to produce a look consistent with the whole page.

most third-party Web advertising, it is used for a range of purposes, from animated rollover buttons to high-quality animated graphics and short cartoons.

Animated GIF is a bitmapped format, which makes it suitable for more subtle effects and textures than vector graphics formats. It is can be the best choice for the animation of artwork made with real or simulated "natural" media. However, it uses a CLUT (color look-up table) of a maximum of 256 colors. Although these can be a subtle custom palette derived from the artwork, many bitmapped images require more for accurate representation. One color from the table may be chosen to be transparent, however, so that animated designs can appear without a bounding box on a Web page, no matter what platform the viewer is using. (Flash allows for this transparency too, but it depends on ActiveX and does not work on a Mac.)

There is no limit to the number of images an animated GIF may contain, but the size of the file can become large and unsuitable for Web use. It uses the lossless LZW compression, which preserves image quality without reducing file sizes. (This compression algorithm has the disadvantage that all software and browser developers have to pay for the right to use it.) In order to achieve a file small enough to download without a long wait, it is necessary to restrict the size of the GIF, and hence the length of the animation.

45

CREATING ANIMATED GIFS

There are many tools available for creating animated GIFs; most of them provide for both the design and the export of the GIF within one application.

The popularity of this format for Web animation is indicated by the wide range of freeware and shareware tools available. At the free end of the spectrum we find tools such as Alan Watts' 16-color program. Available from www.16color.com as a free download for both Windows and Mac platforms, this application provides an interface for creating animated GIFs in 16 colors, and feeds back into his Internet movie machine—a part of the Web site where some 12,000 examples can be seen. By restricting design to bold, aliased pixels in 16 colors, the program ensures that the GIFs remain small and manageable, and that they will play anywhere. It is foolproof and available to anyone.

For designers requiring a more sophisticated tool, ImageReady (now supplied with Photoshop) is an effective solution—especially for those familiar with Photoshop, since it looks similar and offers many of the same facilities. ImageReady works not by creating an image for each frame (a method familiar to anyone who uses Corel Painter), but by using one image document in which a sort of snapshot of the layers at each frame's point is recorded. While this may be confusing for those used to different methods of making animation it soon becomes accessible with practice.

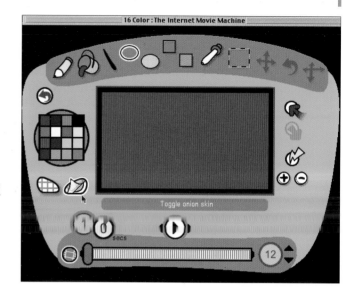

To create a document in ImageReady, we start out with frame 1. We need to create a new layer for this rather than use the background layer. If we add a new frame—frame 2—the artwork in frame 1 will still be showing. Each frame is a sum of the layers at that point, and if the artwork created in frame 1 is not hidden, it is still there in frame 2. There are therefore two ways of creating animation in ImageReady, both exploiting layers. One is appropriate for the creation of traditional frame-by-frame animation, where each frame is drawn from scratch. In this case we need to create a new layer for each new frame and turn off previous layers.

2
Mar@thon, from the 16-color Internet Movie Machine proves that restrictions are not necessarily limitations. The alternating gray and white backgrounds convey an effect of progress with a minimum of means.

1
The 16-color
interface is bold and
cheerful: the drawing
tools and colors are
limited, but the
facilities in this free
application provide all
that is required for
basic animation,
including an onion-
skinning facility, that
toggles on and off.

3
In ImageReady
each frame is a
snapshot of the state
of the Layers palette:
here, at frame 14, all
the other layers
are invisible.

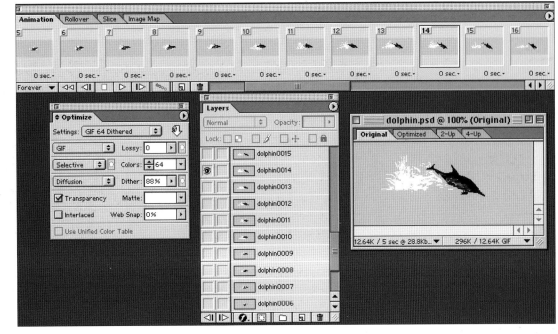

The second exploits the program's distinctive features. Because a frame is a set of layer properties, ImageReady is an excellent tool for creating animation in which those properties change. The easiest property to animate in this way is the position of a layer. By drawing a shape in frame 1 and moving the position of the layer in frame 2, the shape will appear to move. But note that it is the layer that moves; if the object itself is selected and moved then its new position will appear in every frame. Other properties that can be animated are opacity, and parameters for layer effects. For example, an object can fade by decreasing the opacity value for a layer in successive frames, or a drop shadow could rotate around an object and change color by adjusting the parameters for the drop shadow effect frame by frame. By building up layers, with different artwork, and adjusting layer properties for each frame, it is possible to create sophisticated animation. And it is not necessary to do all the work by hand: ImageReady provides a useful tweening facility, which means that for some animation you can create the key frames and have the application do the inbetweening. But tweening can only be applied to layer properties. Any kind of morphing, for example, would have to be drawn by hand.

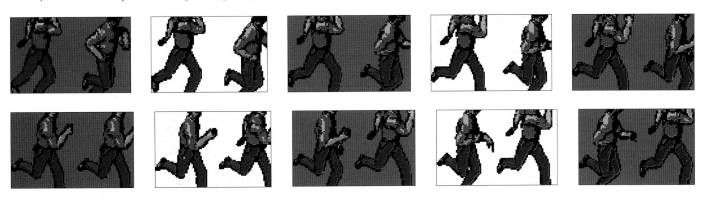

ANIMATED GIF ROLLOVERS

Rollover buttons may use animation in several ways. Because a rollover necessarily involves at least one change of state—from "normal" when nothing is going on, to "over" when the mouse passes over it—some basic animation happens by default if one image is swapped for another on mouse-over. To exploit this potential further, additional images can be used for other states. We could add images for a "click" state, or for two states to represent the "down" and the "up" of the mouse click, and perhaps for an "out" state, when the mouse moves away without having clicked. This means there is the potential for four or five different states in a basic rollover that may be visually related to one another in a more or less obvious way.

This elementary animation, which expresses the functions of a rollover button as well as providing a visual response to the user, may be augmented by turning one or more of the states into a self-contained animation. A rollover could end up as a set of several interrelated animations. There are several ways of doing this, but if the page is controlled with JavaScript it is best to use animated GIFs.

1
At www.gofuse.com Fuse Interactive use animated GIF rollover buttons on their home page.

2 | 3
These zoom effects are achieved in Macromedia Fireworks using 5 frames for each button .

Once again ImageReady provides an easy-to-use interface—for the creation of both static and animated rollover buttons. Having got used to the way that animation is made for an animated GIF, it is necessary to readjust working practices when working with the Rollover palette. In this palette new rollover states are added, rather than new frames, and here each state may be altered without affecting the others, making it possible to animate individual states.

When a new rollover state is added, its type (normal, over, etc.) is indicated above its image in the palette, and may be altered by using a pop-up menu.

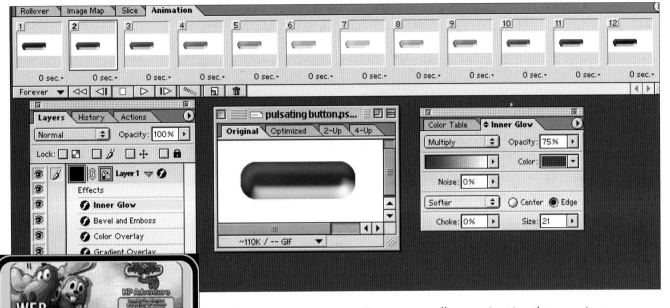

4
In ImageReady a pulsating rollover button can be created by using the Animation and Layers palettes and several layer effects, and then exported as an animated GIF with the rollover functions ready for use.

To create a rollover animation that uses just one image for each state, you can alter each image in turn in the main window. And because ImageReady provides standard Photoshop tools and effects, it is possible to create elaborate effects in this way.

If each individual state is to be animated in itself, the Animation palette is used to create an animated GIF for that state. First, the state must be created in the Rollover palette. With this state selected, we switch to the Animation palette, where the image for the state will be seen in frame 1. From this point on the animation is created as if it were an independent animated GIF. Once the animation for one state is complete, we can switch back to the Rollover palette—where the animated state will still be shown as a single image—and proceed to create further states. ImageReady automatically provides the HTML and JavaScript necessary for actually making the rollovers work on a Web page, so when we preview in the browser the functions of the rollover should all be working as they will on the live Web page.

COMBINING ANIMATED GIFS

Animated GIFs may be combined on a Web page in a number of ways to achieve interesting effects by simple means.

Several different animated GIFs may be placed on the page, independently or within a grid structure. This sets up an interaction between the different animations that can produce a whole greater than the sum of the parts. If the GIFs are all set to loop "forever," and they are not all the same length, there will be a large number of permutations. This is therefore a quick and easy way of creating a constantly changing display.

However, this will be tedious for the viewer unless the loops are long and the artwork complex. To create greater variety, animated GIFs can be swapped in place of one another, or in substitution for still images. They can be made to start after a delay, or vanish if replaced by a still matching the background. They can also move across a Web page; this is particularly effective for small

50

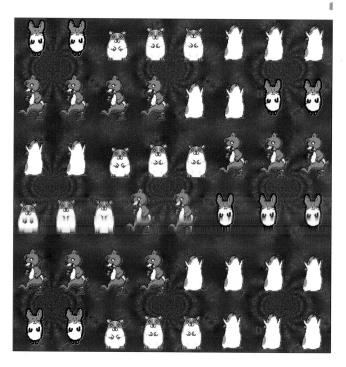

2

1
www.hampsterdance2.com combines and repeats a set of four animated GIFs for a unique result.

2 | 3 | 4
A butterfly flaps its wings over a flower at www.precinct.net. This is achieved by using an image sliced into parts—still GIFs plus an animated one for the butterfly.

3

"Stay here, here is good."

looped elements with transparent backgrounds. In this way, for example, we could make a walking figure cross the screen, by moving a looping animated GIF of a walk cycle. All of these time-based events and movements are achieved by using JavaScript, and are discussed in the following pages.

Another way of combining animated GIFS, or combining animated GIF elements with still elements, is to use image slicing. This was designed to enable different parts of a large image to be optimized separately, for the sake of small file sizes. It is not even necessary for all the parts to be in the same file format, so the subject could be saved as a JPEG at a high-quality setting, and other slices at lower settings or as GIFs. They are all put back together by the HTML on the Web page, and appear—once they have all downloaded—as a single image. Because the viewer would see the slices assemble as the page downloads, it is desirable to conceal the assembly behind a layer that becomes invisible once the page is fully loaded.

Slicing is of great value in Web animation. If an image is large, it will become much larger if it is all animated in every frame of an animated GIF. Savings in file sizes can be achieved by slicing the image to isolate those parts to be animated, for example, the butterfly that flaps its wings over a static flower at

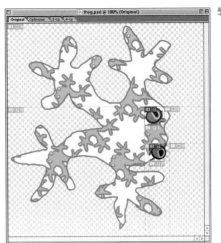

5
ImageReady allows us to slice an image and then animate the slices. Here, the eyes of the frog have been separated. Since these are only a tiny part of the whole, animating just these slices is more economical if we want a frog with swiveling eyes.

www.precinct.net. ImageReady makes this process easy through the use of its slicing tools (also available in Photoshop). A single large image may be sliced by making marquee selections with the dagger slicing tool from the Tools palette. The program creates all the other slices required to define the whole image. You can work on the slice using ImageReady's Animation palette providing that the slice is placed on a layer of its own.

Alternatively, you can open the slices as separate files and turn each into an animated GIF. The results must be saved as replacements for the original still files. If it does not have the same name and is not in the same place as the file that we started with, the HTML will not be able to reconstruct it in the browser.

4

INTRODUCING JAVASCRIPT

HTML—HyperText Markup Language—is the foundation of all Web pages. But it is only concerned with document structure, not layout, and provides no response to user input other than to go to another page or site via a link. Much of what we see and do on a Web site, therefore, cannot be specified in HTML alone. So HTML has been extended by the use of programming in JavaScript (and VBScript for Windows) and Cascading Style Sheets (CSS). The combination of these elements is referred to as Dynamic HTML (DHTML). For animation designers it is JavaScript that is of interest.

JavaScript allows Web pages to act as event-driven systems—a vital concept that we make use of all the time on desktop computers, even if we give it little thought. In the early days of computing systems, a program would prompt a user for a response. What we now think of as standard interactive interface elements, such as rollovers, did not exist in these systems. We are very used to working with event-driven systems in our own computers, with sophisticated desktops and applications that have drop-down menus, drag-and-drop, tool selection, and other luxuries. But it's different on the World Wide Web. Without JavaScript, Web pages that do not use an alternative could only present a fixed display with static links to click on, which is just how many Web pages still behave.

JavaScript detects events and changes elements of the document structure in a Web page. This means that by using JavaScript we can detect mouse states and some key-presses. And we can make things happen in response, for example, we can swap images or animated GIFs, or alter the display of the page. The range of events JavaScript can detect is defined in the HTML Standard, and is limited. For a more elaborate response it is necessary to use a plug-in such as Flash or Shockwave, or to write programs in Java proper. However, most of the basic functions of Web pages can be handled in JavaScript, and, combined with interesting artwork, it can do a good job without any plug-ins.

JavaScript detects an event initiated by the user, which triggers a script that changes the page. Among the elements of a Web page are its images. By changing the source attributes of these elements, JavaScript enables us to replace one image—including an animated GIF—with another one. This is how all rollover and related functions work in JavaScript. Even if the images are stills, basic animation occurs during this replacement. Therefore this is a kind of user-driven animation, which, if used for many rollover points on a page, can build into something elaborate.

It is now rarely necessary for designers to know how to write JavaScript. Most of the usual Web-page operations can be selected in programs such as GoLive and Dreamweaver, and the rest follows automatically. We are still using JavaScript, but it is hidden from our view, unless we dive beneath the surface to see what is going on.

53

1 | 2
This site at www.randommedia.co.uk, is written in DHTML. The lines and text that run across the center of the page move up and down, and the menu window is draggable. The rollovers use image replacement.

3
Volkswagen's Web page at www.beetle.de echoes the curves of the car itself and the bubbly image that reflects the popular perception of the car. With a lot of white space and the use of light colors, everything floats in the space—all based on JavaScript.

3

IMAGE SWAPPING AND REMOTE ROLLOVERS

Much of the animation that JavaScript enables is image swapping. One image or animated GIF is replaced by another. This allows us to design rollovers, remote rollovers, and nonfunctional in-place image swaps in the form of slide shows.

As unsophisticated as it sounds, a slide show can be useful, for example, displaying a sequence of satellite images showing cloud cover over a period of time. It is suited to this, since the viewer needs time to understand the information in each frame. But this kind of presentation cannot play very fast so it is not suitable for animation, which requires smooth transitions and flow; an animated GIF would be a better choice here.

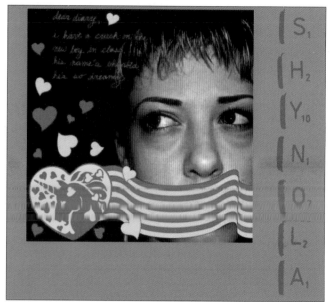

1

There are no obvious buttons or menu items on the DHTML welcome page at www.shynola.co.uk. Only one element responds to the user—a rollover button, which is part of the overall design. When the mouse rolls over the heart and unicorn, the colors are reversed by a straight image swap.

2

Shynola's main page uses a remote rollover that appears as a text and image box to the right of the yellow truck. This is a layer that is only visible when activated by a rollover button in the form of a speaker icon lower down the page.

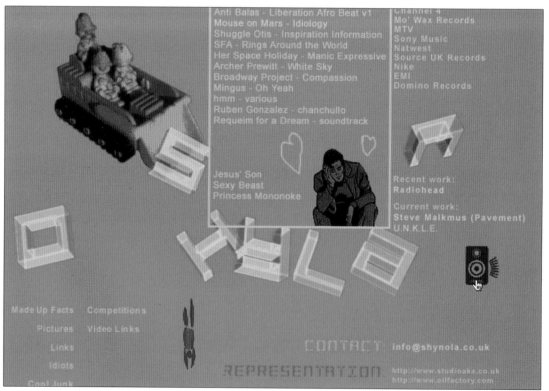

3 | 4
When the mouse rolls over areas of the floor plan at www.gofuse.com, image swapping provides a photo of that part of the interior in the main window, and descriptive text appears above the plan.

JavaScript effectively achieves both in-place and remote rollovers, thus allowing a freedom of design for the functional elements without using Flash or similar technologies. A remote rollover is one where the image or animation displayed as a result of a mouse-over does not show up on the same spot, but elsewhere on the page. (A remote rollover is often used in conjunction with an ordinary rollover, so that two changes occur.)

It is important to remember that JavaScript swaps images—there has to be something to be swapped with. On many Web pages that use remote rollovers it is not possible to see this initial element—its invisibility is what makes it so effective. The element to be swapped out has to be positioned in the right place, and, if it is not a transparent GIF it ought to be of identical pixel dimensions at screen resolution (still taken to be 72dpi) as the element to be swapped in. To create remote rollovers that pop up out of nowhere, therefore, it is necessary to use a still image placeholder that is either a totally transparent GIF, an exact copy of the part of the background on which it sits, or a slice of an image on

which a new slice will appear. The visual responses to rolling over different items may appear in the same place on the page or in different places.

A remote rollover can also turn a still image into an animation. In this case the element to be swapped out should either be a still image of the first frame of an animated GIF, which is replaced by the animation upon mouse-over, or an image not taken from the animation at all. This second option is preferable, because if an animated GIF has been preloaded with the page it may not start playing at its first frame when swapped in.

What has been swapped in must also be swapped out if the mouse moves away from the rollover point ('mouseout') without clicking. The normal state is not reinstated automatically—it is necessary to use JavaScript to detect and act on mouse-over and mouseout events. This means that when mouseout is detected, either the original image is reinstated, or a new image or animated GIF is swapped in.

TIME-BASED JAVASCRIPT ACTIONS

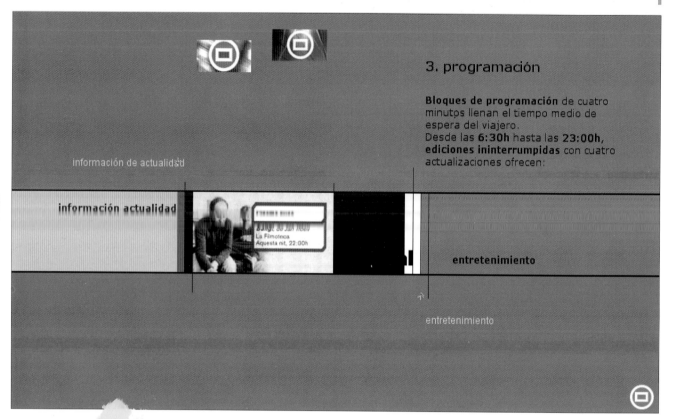

While some JavaScript animation occurs in response to input from the user, other kinds of visual activity may be purely time-based.

Once a Web page has loaded it begins its existence in time, which will continue until the viewer leaves. It is possible to define points in this time base—albeit not as accurately as by a clock—at which things, including animation, will happen. These are not triggered events like rollovers, but are controlled by scripts putting themselves to sleep for some time, and then waking up to do something. If we use Web-authoring programs such as Dreamweaver and GoLive it will not be apparent that this is how it works, since the coding is done for us.

We can use JavaScript to start or stop an animation after a while, to swap animations and still images in and

1 | 2
The upper left part of this DHTML page at www.canalmetro.net has a changing display of picture windows that pop up in pairs across the space in different arrangements. Over time this animation uses all of this otherwise blank area.

out at specified points in time, to control the speed of a coordinated slide show, to control animations playing together, or to sequence animations in different slices of a sliced image. We need to remember that this concept of time is a loose one. Because of the variables involved when displaying material on the Internet, the timings of a DHTML Web page are approximate.

In programs like Dreamweaver and GoLive, a timeline is provided to assist with design of the page. However, both its terminology and appearance may be misleading, especially to animators used to working with

2

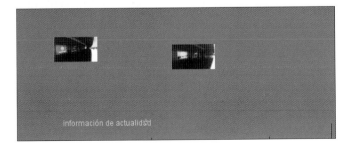

timelines in other contexts. In Dreamweaver, for example, the timeline is presented in "frames," and a rate of frames per second (fps) may be set. But these are not frames in the normal animation sense; they are arbitrary conceptual divisions of time.

Although a Web page's existence in time may start once the page is fully loaded, it may have more than one timeline as defined in these programs, none of which need start immediately. Each timeline has a fixed extent defined by the point at which the last object in it ends. The extent of the timeline is therefore wholly unrelated to the length of time a user visits the page. You can think of each timeline as a kind of movie—a self-contained set of things going on at specified points in time. A timeline may be set to start the instant the page has loaded (autoplay), it may start after a delay, or it can be triggered by an event such as a mouse-over. A timeline can be set to loop and even contain instructions to start up additional timelines at specified points.

To control document elements on a timeline we need to set key frames—specific points at which something will happen. In JavaScript we are limited as to what we can control in this way. At a key frame we can swap an image or animated GIF (adjusting the image source), or control the visibility, z-order (front to back ordering of layers), or the positioning of layers (known as 'floating boxes' in GoLive). In this context a layer is an area on the Web page for which we can set position, size, and visibility; it can contain the same document elements as can the main body of the document.

With advances in Flash and Shockwave these operations are carried out less frequently in DHTML. But this is still entirely adequate, and the genesis of Web authoring programs like Dreamweaver and GoLive, in which the JavaScript is neatly packaged so that it can be picked and added to a timeline, has made this technology easier for designers to use.

57

MOVING AROUND WITH DHTML

DHTML can move document elements around a Web page by using JavaScript with CSS. A movable element is a <div> or a <span> in HTML terms: these are shown in GoLive as floating boxes and in Dreamweaver as layers. These elements contain familiar document elements, such as images, animated GIFs, and text—and it is the movement of the visual elements that we actually see. Because <div>s and <span>s are the only HTML document elements that can be positioned absolutely on the page, they are the only ones that can be moved. Anything that we want to see move across the page, therefore, must be placed within a <div> or a <span>.

Aardman Animations Ltd. provides an excellent example of movement using DHTML, on their Web pages at www.aardman. com/showcase, featuring the character Morph. The page was created in GoLive, and the effect is achieved very simply. Here Morph is an animated GIF, looping over just five frames. The animation shows him balancing on a rolling battery, wobbling and waving his arms. The animated GIF crosses the page from upper right to lower left during the course of 100 GoLive frames at a rate of 15 fps, giving a convincing impression of Morph traveling across the page. The whole movement is looped, so that when he reaches the bottom he starts once again from the top. It is the combination of the animated GIF with the DHTML animation of the whole element across the page that makes this so successful.

It is not difficult to create such an effect using GoLive. First, we position a floating box at the starting position in the Layout window,

Morph rolls across the screen in an animated GIF of five frames, with a transparent background. His shadow adds a subtle touch of realism.

and place the animated GIF (or other element) in it. Creating this floating box automatically places a key frame at the beginning of a new track in the Timeline window. We then move to the point in the timeline where we want the movement to stop—frame 100 in the case of Morph—and insert a new key frame there. With the edit line over this final key frame in the Timeline window, we return to the Layout window and drag our floating box to the position where we want the movement to end. The skill lies in the creation of appropriate artwork, and the judgement of the amount of distance to cross in the specified time to produce the effect. As master animators Aardman have judged this to perfection, and the result is exactly like a version of an original Morph movement on TV. The way this character's movements have been tailored to fit the constraints and technologies of the Internet without any loss of quality is a flawless exercise in Web animation done with the basic technologies of the animated GIF and DHTML.

Movements achieved with DHTML do not need to follow a single straight path. The path may be broken up into many sections by inserting additional key frames on the timeline, with a change of direction possible at each key frame. And a path between any two points may be interpolated as a bézier curve instead of a straight line. When using Dreamweaver and GoLive it is even possible to drag the floating box (or layer) around in the Layout window and have the program record the path to create key frames on the timeline automatically.

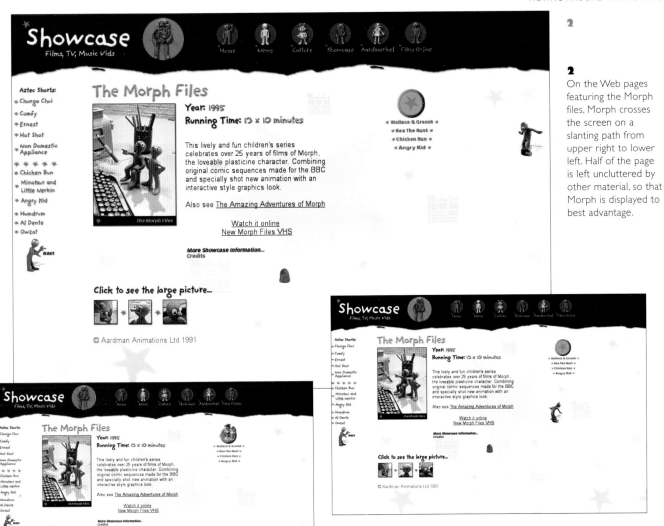

2
On the Web pages featuring the Morph files, Morph crosses the screen on a slanting path from upper right to lower left. Half of the page is left uncluttered by other material, so that Morph is displayed to best advantage.

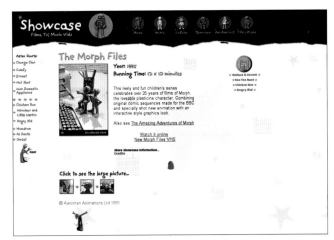

Animation of an element across a Web page can be extremely effective if used with appropriate material, but this technique should be used with discretion. It can work well with text elements in some contexts, with abstract graphic elements in an overall design, and with animated GIFs. But a still image sliding around on the screen needs a good reason to do so. Care should be taken to avoid using this kind of animation gratuitously.

ADVANCED DHTML ANIMATION

Although JavaScript is powerful enough for any kind of computation, it has serious limitations as a tool for animation on Web pages. It can only manipulate page elements that have already been created elsewhere. Visual elements such as still images and animated GIFs have to be predesigned in another application, and DHTML cannot get inside those elements to alter them. Compared with Flash and Macromedia Director, which allow designers to combine work on content creation with design and control of the actions in an integrated way, DHTML is restrictive, relatively clumsy, and requires programming skills for anything advanced.

Web-authoring applications like Dreamweaver and GoLive only provide a limited set of prefabricated JavaScript actions. Because DHTML is extensible it allows designers to include other ready-made custom actions, but to achieve anything original it is necessary to write the JavaScript by hand. This requires programming knowledge, and it can be laborious because different versions are needed for the site to work on different browsers, and switching code is required to make the changeovers. Because browsers are not able to implement DHTML properly, errors frequently occur, making the display of the page problematic and unreliable.

www.bratta.com and the experimental version 1 of testphase.at/medialab are examples of animation hand-coded in DHTML. We can only admire the skills and tenacity involved in producing work in this way. Both of these sites have managed to conceal the fact that

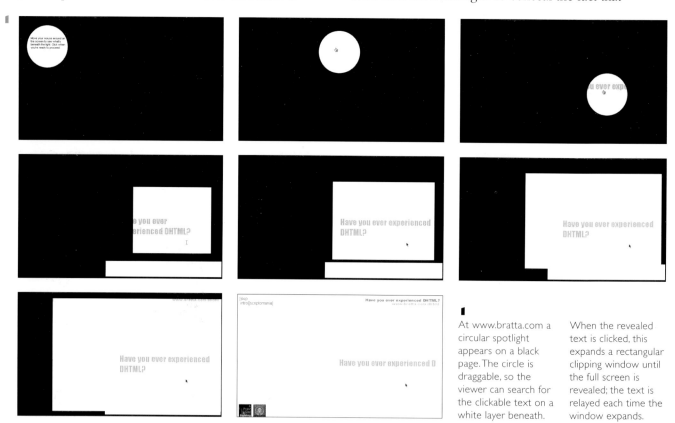

At www.bratta.com a circular spotlight appears on a black page. The circle is draggable, so the viewer can search for the clickable text on a white layer beneath.

When the revealed text is clicked, this expands a rectangular clipping window until the full screen is revealed; the text is relayed each time the window expands.

JavaScript cannot get inside the animation, and they play much as though they were made with plug-in technologies. However, for many designers it would be easier to use Flash or Director. The DHTML version of the medialab site was created when today's plug-in technologies were not ready for this kind of work. This was highly advanced work in DHTML at the time. But now a new version of the same work, made as Shockwave, is available on the same site. Shockwave resolves all the problems that were inherent in using DHTML, and adds a smooth interface. It is particularly instructive to compare the two versions because they both deal with the same manipulated elements.

In a couple of years' time DHTML may seem a much more attractive option for advanced and unusual Web animation than it does today. It has an official status that the plug-in technologies lack—there are WWW Consortium Recommendations covering all of the DHTML elements, and, although browsers do not currently implement these properly, in the future they may do so. It is also probable that packages like Dreamweaver and GoLive will continue to develop and expand their range of JavaScript actions making more advanced DHTML animation techniques available to those without programming skills. Web authoring packages like these have already made life much easier for designers. However, by definition DHTML will still be limited to the manipulation of predesigned elements, which means that certain kinds of animation will always be beyond its scope.

2
The first version of digital medialab, at testphase.at, was hand-coded in DHTML. This interactive work presents different permutations of faces and bodies that change and rotate, according to input from the user.

JAVA ECONOMY

The writing of Java programs or applets is not for the technically timid or uninitiated. Most Java is written by professional programmers. Fortunately for animators and designers, however, many Java applets have been made available to the public for free downloading. These applets are often supported with helpful notes, for those without programming experience.

Animation controlled by Java can be unusual, including interactivity, or simple and functional. And because the animation is achieved by manipulating a few images with a short program, it involves small file sizes relative to the complexity of the animation. Java animation is both effective and economical.

In the example illustrated, a free Java applet, ChompText, has been applied to the title of this book. The applet is imported into a Web-authoring application such as Dreamweaver or GoLive, and parameters for background and text color are entered, as is the text

1
Ready-made Java applets enable Java animations to be customized. The banner window is positioned on the page, and parameter values are entered in the dialog box.

2
The three sprite faces of the chomper are GIFs with a transparent background, which allow the custom background and text to show up.

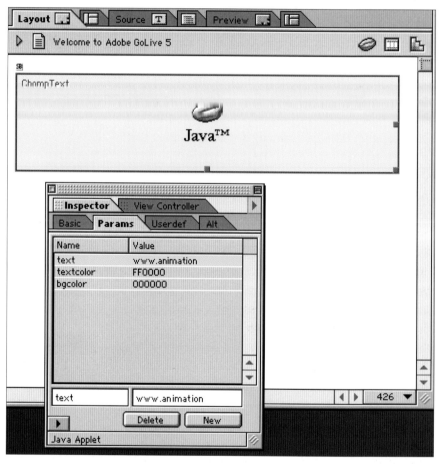

2
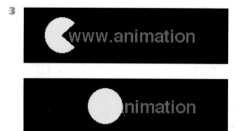

3

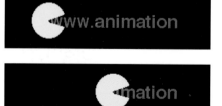

which is to be chomped. The applet uses three sprite faces, animation states that are supplied when the applet is downloaded. The applet substitutes these faces in turn as the chomper moves across the banner, eating the text that lies in its path.

It is possible to express movements mathematically, and so to create sophisticated animations entirely in Java. However, when the model becomes more complex than the real thing, we should throw the model away. In practice it is far easier to create the basic elements of the animation by hand, and to use programming only to control changes and interactivity. This is what Karl Hörnell has done in his animation of a frog eating flies at www.javaonthebrain.com. He uses sprite faces to show eight different states of the frog's head and three views of a fly, which, with the image of the whole frog, are stored in a single still GIF. This is downloaded with the page, and the animation is done by a Java applet on the viewer's computer. The flies come into existence randomly, as do their flight paths. The frog sits quietly breathing, by means of sprite face substitution of his head, until a fly approaches closely. When a fly enters the critical zone the frog's mouth opens. At this point the Java applet is used to draw a simple tongue-catching-a-fly animation. As soon as this is complete the animation returns to sprite face substitution.

By combining random-value generation for movements, real-time algorithmic graphics for the tongue, and sprite face substitution for the frog's head movements, an animation is created which is almost limitlessly variable, although based on just twelve drawings. For this kind of job, Java is the perfect tool.

3

ChompText is crude perhaps, but effective nonetheless. Indeed, as a reminder of the 1970s computer game it is designed to be so. As the chomper makes its voracious journey across the banner, the text behind the sprite is masked out until the animation is completed and loops back to the beginning.

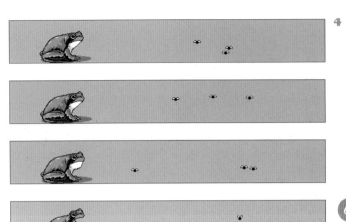

4 | 5
The froggy applet is free to download and can be embedded in any Web page, with the colors set according to personal choice. The frog's head has been animated by hand, but the rest is done by computation.

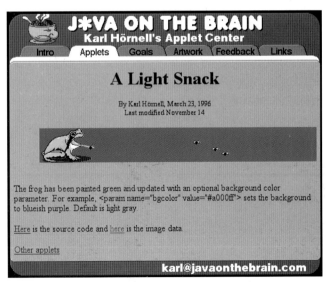

JAVA EFFECTS

The Java AWT (Abstract Window Toolkit) allows programs to create image objects, and manipulate image data. To a Java program, an image is simply an array of pixel values, which can be manipulated like any other values. What this means for Web animation is that Java—and only Java—allows us to take images apart, pixel by pixel, and do things to them. This is done by sending a Java applet to the user's computer, where it works in situ in a fast and economical way.

Java enables the creation of custom effects—similar to Photoshop filters—by hand-coding. A programmer is needed to write these applets, but not to use them; there are many available for free download. One of the most popular Java applets for applying special effects to a still image is David Griffiths' Lake, available for free from www.demon.co.uk/davidg and other Java sites. This applet turns half of a still picture (in GIF or JPEG format) into a rippling water effect, e.g., by adding a rippling reflection effect to everything below a point set as the "horizon." It creates and loops a sequence of 12 frames from one image. It calculates a transposition of some pixels up or down in each frame in a pattern modeled on a sine wave (to simulate ripples on the water's surface) and then replaces the image it used for that calculation with the new version to get the next frame.

It is often by using the knowledge of physical properties and effects, such as the way water ripples or drops act on a surface, that the Java applets controlling

animations can be made so effective. These sorts of functions are easy to express mathematically, and the piece of code to be downloaded to the user's machine is small. Once again it is computation that makes a still become a moving animation.

3

4

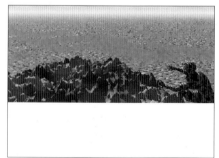

5

1 | 2
The Lake applet may be applied to an image that already contains water, whether real or computer generated. Here, image 1 is the original still JPEG, and image 2 has the effect applied and working. The "horizon" in the applet is set where the water meets the land, so that only the water moves. This turns a Bryce still into an animation that will play well with a small download.

Java-effects animation is not limited to art or games. It is now finding its way into commercial Web animation design. For example, Freestyle Interactive has produced some impressive Java banner ads for Hewlett Packard and other clients. The HP Invent algorithm ad is created by constant computation of a time-varying plot of a 3D surface. This is defined by an equation which is part of the ad and whose coefficients the viewer can alter by clicking. This interactivity, and the resulting changes in the animation, are remarkable in the context of a banner advertisement and serve to demonstrate another aspect of the future for Java animation on the Web.

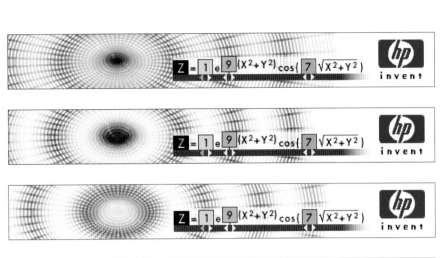

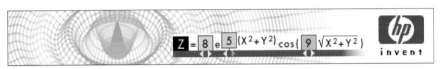

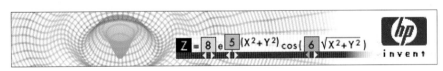

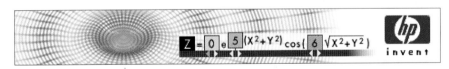

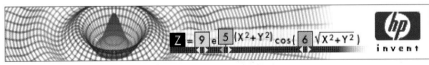

3 | 4 | 5 | 6
If a "horizon" is set in the Lake applet, the image size remains the same and no reflection is created: ripple is applied to the lower half of the image (4). This can be useful where there is no water to start with. In image 5 the original (3) was cropped and the applet applied without a horizon, (5) thus adding a rippling reflection onto the bottom of the image (6), which is quite different from the result in 4.

7
The HP Invent Algorithm banner ad uses Java to compute a varying animation set according to parameters that the viewer can change.

JAVA INTERACTIVITY

In Java it is a small step from an animation which only plays, to adding interactivity that allows the viewer to control what happens. Any Java applet using the AWT (Abstract Window Toolkit) can receive all the mouse and keystroke events. Because AWT provides a flexible framework for writing code to handle these events, it is possible for a Java applet to do anything that any computer program can do in response to user input— except things that are forbidden, such as writing to the user's disk. This means that Java is the most powerful tool for interactive animation on the Web—but to exploit it fully requires professional programming.

At the simplest level of interactivity, an applet like PoolMenu will apply an effect to an image in response to a mouse event. When the mouse is held over a part of the image for a short length of time an effect appears— starting from the mouse's position—like the ripples observed when a drop falls onto the surface of water. In this case, the animation must be calculated by the applet in real-time, in response to user input. When applying effects applets like this one to our own images it is necessary to ensure that the image is appropriate for the effect involved.

Interactivity is taken a step further at www.sodaplay.com, which allows the construction and interactive animation of objects or creatures. This is not only graphically pleasing, but educational and a lot of fun. It is also an effective demonstration of the power of Java for interactivity. The models respond beautifully to interaction by mouse and have additional parameters, such as gravity, which can be turned on or off, with immediate results. Computation of the physical properties of masses, springs, and muscles, taken together with the principle of emergent behavior (which means that a system can be more complex than the elements that combined to produce it) gives a result that

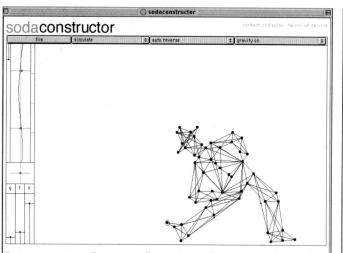

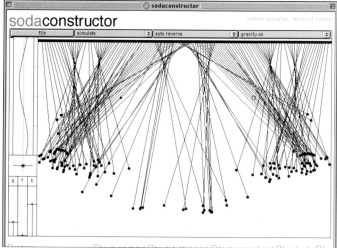

1

PoolMenu uses a Java
applet to generate
ripples where the
mouse rests.

is compelling. The visitor can even
build custom models out of the
basic physical elements, rather like
an online Meccano set come to life.

Another example of advanced
interactive Java animation is Open
Studio, found at draw.artcontext.net.
This is a complete mini-application
that downloads and runs inside the
browser, giving the user a custom
interface including controls over
color and some unusual drawing
tools. The applet maintains a two-
way connection with the host
server, so that a record of what the
user draws is recorded. All recent
drawings can be accessed so that
they redraw themselves on the
user's screen. Up to nine users can
be connected through the server at
once, allowing for real multiparty
interactive animation. The power of
this applet, which only takes a
minute to download, is impressive
and this could not be achieved
without serious Java programming.

4 | 5 | 6

Open Studio, created
by Andy Deck, runs as
a Java applet in the
user's browser. It
features a wide range
of unusual drawing
tools, color control,
and playback of
interactive
animations.

2 | 3

At the
www.sodaplay.com
site the sophisticated
model construction,
animation, and

interactivity are
enabled by Java,
resulting in a wide
variety of models
and animations.

67

INTRODUCING FLASH

Flash is the foremost application for creating SWF files—Flash movies—for the Internet. All SWF files require Macromedia's Flash Player plug-in before they can be played, but Flash (the program) no longer has a monopoly on their creation. Flash started as an animation tool for vector graphics; it produced unusually compact output for moving images. Scripting support was added to the animation capabilities, and it can now achieve interactivity and other advanced functions. Although primarily a vector graphics application, Flash can work with bitmapped images, and may sometimes produce more impressive results than, for example, QuickTime.

Flash uses a Timeline with multiple layers, which may be locked or invisible, and on which frames are inserted at every point where there is created (or imported) content. The material itself is created and manipulated on the stage, which is a window similar to those used for drawing etc. in design applications. The frame size and frame rate are specified on starting a new project, although the frame rate can be changed by selecting Movie under the Modify menu.

The concept of key frames used in Flash is the classic one from traditional animation. If the designer is creating an animation by drawing each frame by hand, then every frame is a key frame. If inbetweening is used, the key frames are those that the designer

creates, and between which the tweening is to occur. Flash provides two kinds of automatic tweening: motion tweening and shape tweening—otherwise known as morphing. Motion tweening could be used, for example, to move an object across the stage, and for more elaborate movements it is possible to create a motion path. But despite the name, motion tweening can also be used to tween properties other than motion: specifically size, orientation, fill color and opacity. These facilities can be extremely useful when creating subtle animation.

Shape tweening is used for automated transformations, for example, to morph a circle into a star, or a duck into a horse. Unfortunately, although shape tweening is fun to use, it is highly processor intensive, and can cause very slow playback or stuttering, especially if applied in multiple layers. Motion tweening, on the other hand, is very efficient.

2 | 3
London's South Bank Centre also relies on Flash's ability to work with bitmapped images. Many pages at main.sbc.org.uk use imagery derived from photographic originals.

1
Flash is not restricted to vector graphics artwork. At www.switcheroozoo.com photographic images are used for interactive transformations.

4
Flash uses a timeline with multiple layers; the key frames are identified by black dots. Tweening is indicated by arrows and color tints—mauve for motion; green for shape.

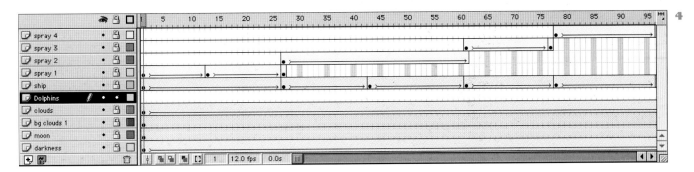

SIMPLE FLASH MOVIES

Many designers find that Flash is the best tool for the creation of straightforward motion graphics animation on the Web. It is quick and easy to use, can produce elegant results that are economical in download time, and are very reliable. Sometimes its capacity to produce simple but effective results is overlooked in an attempt to be technologically sophisticated. This is a pity because it is very often an understanding of the program's essential nature that leads to the most effective work.

Flash handles simple shapes and colors well, producing smooth animation. With a tool like this, it is often the case that less is more. This is well demonstrated by the sparse style of work on Joshua Davis' experimental Web sites, www.praystation.com and www.once-upon-a-forest.com, which show a thorough understanding of Flash's strengths, and limitations.

We do not need to create a whole site with Flash in order to take advantage of its potential. A SWF file may be imported into a Web-authoring application and positioned as if it were a still image. It is therefore possible to incorporate discrete Flash elements into a Web page that contains other types of material. In this way Flash may be used as a self-contained animated element, as well as for interactive elements such as menu bars. However, it is not possible to move a Flash element around on the page with DHTML as we can an animated GIF, nor can we reliably control the start and stop of the Flash movie with DHTML. We are therefore limited if Flash is combined with non-Flash elements.

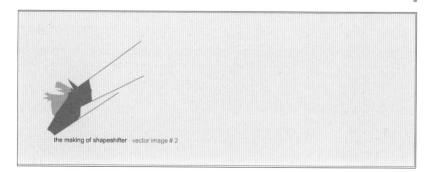

the making of shapeshifter · vector image # 2

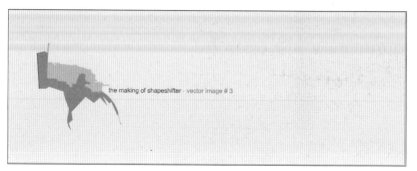

the making of shapeshifter · vector image # 3

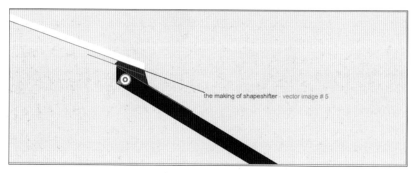

the making of shapeshifter · vector image # 5

Because Flash produces such smooth vector-graphics animation, it is frequently used for webisodes and other presentations of cartoons on the Web. Although it is capable of much more subtle and elegant graphics, it is also well suited to the bold shapes and colors typical of this type of material—and in this case the use of "brash Flash" may well be justified. At present it is probably the premier delivery format for cartoons over the Internet, and many cartoon animators are now specializing in the creation of Flash animation.

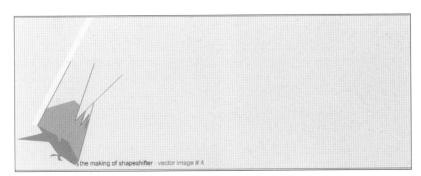

the making of shapeshifter · vector image # 4

1
Much of the work at
www.praystation.com
demonstrates the
power of graphic
simplicity in Flash,
although it often uses
advanced scripting to
drive the animation.

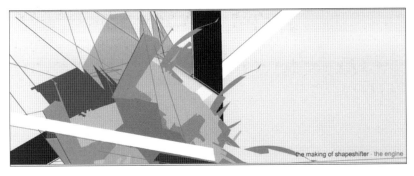

the making of shapeshifter · the engine

3
www.wildbrain.com
shows webisodes
over the Internet in
the form of simple
Flash movies.

3

2

2
www.once-upon-a-
forest.com is an
experimental site that
exploits and reveals
Flash's strengths.

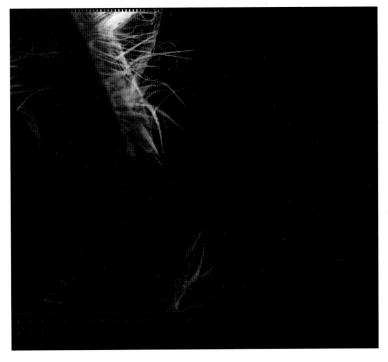

STREAMING FLASH

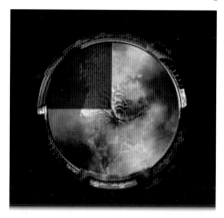

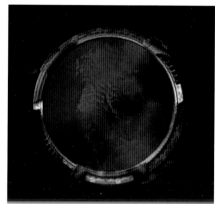

Flash is a streamed format, which means that it plays each frame as it arrives over the Internet and nothing can alter that characteristic. However, we can work with and around it. This is necessary because low-bandwidth connections are not sufficiently fast to download and play back the frames at a satisfactory rate in real-time. Since we cannot just tell Flash not to start playing until all frames are downloaded, we have to use scripts to control it.

It is usual, with large Flash movies that take a while to download, to have a sequence at the beginning of the SWF that is simple and will download almost instantly—a preloading sequence. A script is attached to the final frame of this sequence, instructing it to continue looping until a certain frame in the main movie has loaded. This critical frame may well be the final one, but in more complicated Flash presentations it may not be.

When the script attached to the preloading sequence finds that the specified critical frame has loaded, it either plays the main movie or it shows a frame or short looping sequence inviting the user to click to start playback. This is a better option than commencing playback automatically because the user's attention may have wandered during the download process.

Because the download of a large Flash movie can take several minutes, it is important to let the viewer know that something is happening, and that the page is being accessed. It is not, therefore, a good idea to use one static frame during the loading process—a sequence that is obviously alive is reassuring to the user. A refinement of this is adding a progress bar into the pre-loading sequence. This is complex to achieve, but comforting to the viewer waiting to see the main movie.

1
Each stage of the Flash game at www.lego.com/matanui has to be loaded as the user moves through the scenes. The rotating area of shadow on this circular map indicates activity, but not the extent of progress.

2
There is no reason why progress should be measured as a bar. This progress animation at www.wmteam.de is consistent with the design of the site, yet conveys a clear message to the viewer.

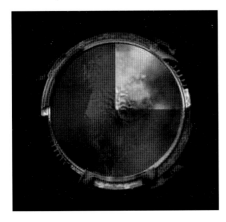

3
At the Web site for
FlashForward 2001
in NYC, loading is
indicated by a moving
stream of arrows, and
animation of the text,
but no measure of
loading progress.

In order to create a progress bar animation, we have to create a movie clip symbol of something progressing. Although this animation needs to show a measure of progress in some way, it is not necessary that it look like a conventional progress bar in an operating system. However, if we wish to keep the viewer informed, we should make sure that the graphic message is intelligible.

73

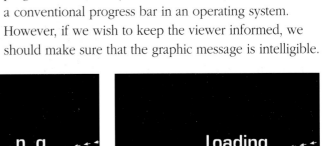

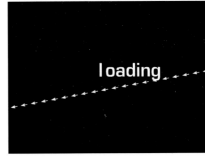

3

4
www.babylonheadbox.
fsnet.co.uk uses a
complementary
animation overlaid on
the main screen while

the Web page proper
is loading, together
with a clear
statement of progress
for the viewer.

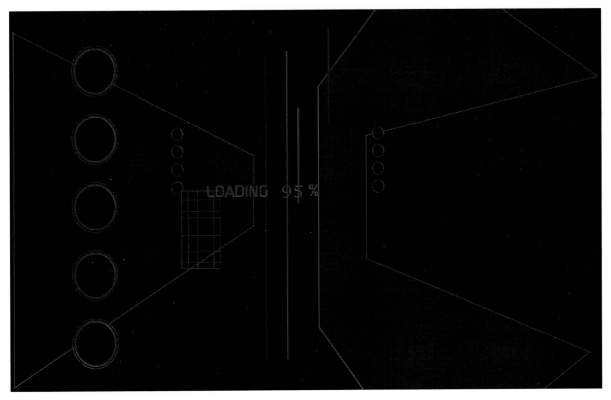

4

COMPLEX FLASH MOVIES

  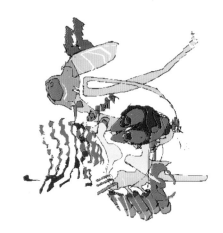

To create Flash movies more complex than an animation that just plays through from start to finish, we create movies within movies. It may be desirable to do this either to build up a more varied animation, or to accommodate different animated elements within a single Flash Web page.

To achieve these richer Flash designs we use instances of movie-clip symbols. Any piece of animation, with or without scripting attached, may be used as a movie-clip symbol, but as it is laborious to convert a preexisting animation sequence to a symbol, it is preferable to create a new symbol each time we make a self-contained movie clip to use in a larger movie.

Movie-clip symbols are held in the Library, and can be dragged on to the stage any number of times. Each time one is dragged on to the stage a new instance of that symbol is created. The same movie clip can be reused many times, in different positions on the stage and Timeline. It is advisable to name each instance, so that it can be referred to from any script we wish to run, and so it can be made to do things like start, stop, or duplicate itself. By using just a few movie-clip symbols— a small set of self-contained animations—it is possible to create much from little. This can be done in response to user input, and thus be interactive, but it can also be valuable in Flash animation that plays on its own. Some sophisticated uses of this will require writing Flash 5 ActionScript by hand, or using someone else's pre-written scripts.

There are only two ways a Flash movie can develop in a nonlinear way—through interactive response to user input, or by using its random-number generator. Where a movie made up of movie-clip symbols is playing, and continuously changing in an apparently infinite pattern of development, either its creator was enormously patient and preprogrammed a large piece of work from a few elements, or random number generation is being used. The use of random numbers in conjunction with advanced scripting creates rich animation by economical means. We can create a set of movie-clip symbols, and leave the choreography of the animation to the scripts, without doing more than ensuring that an instance of each clip is available on the stage. Scripting can make these instances visible or invisible, start and stop them, make them jump to a specific frame and then play or stop, duplicate them or get rid of duplicates, or move them around and alter their z-ordering (front to back overlay). A designer can create an animation in which even they will not be able to foresee how it will look and play.

1
This complex Flash animation seen at www.presstube.com uses multiple instances of movie-clip symbols.

2

Movies within movies are used when a whole page is created in Flash and different things need to happen on it. By using instances of movie clip symbols we can have different animated elements that work independently of one another. For example, a small animated sequence might loop in one corner of the page all the time that the page is displayed, no matter what else is going on. Movie-clip symbols may be instructed to play up to a certain critical frame, and then stop until further activated by user input. A new movie can be loaded into an instance of a movie-clip symbol, allowing the inclusion of new material not part of the main movie that is fetched from the server. This makes it possible to break down a movie into separate parts, so that each movie clip is only downloaded if and when it is needed.

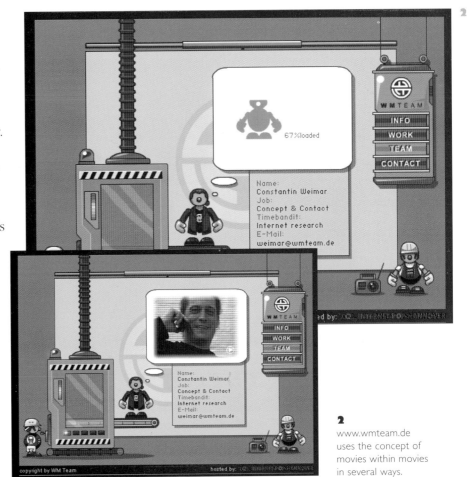

2
www.wmteam.de uses the concept of movies within movies in several ways.

SIMPLE INTERACTIVITY IN FLASH

There are now many Web sites constructed entirely with Flash. Most of these require the normal functional elements to be delivered in Flash. Also, it is not uncommon for sites created in HTML to use SWF elements together with other technologies, and here again Flash may be used for the functional parts. The advantages of Flash in this situation include its facility for animation, the ease with which interactive elements can be created, the compact size of vector graphics, and avoiding the use of DHTML.

To respond to mouse or keyboard events from the user, it is essential that there is some element present that can receive events. In Flash, the only things that can do this are button symbols and movie-clip symbols. A button symbol, for example, might be an invisible (fully transparent) element the size of the whole stage, which filled the background. This would mean that a mouse click on any point not obscured by other elements further forward, or further up in the hierarchy of layers, would activate the button.

Scripts activated by user input can control what happens in a Flash movie in two ways. They can do things which affect the whole movie—such as start or

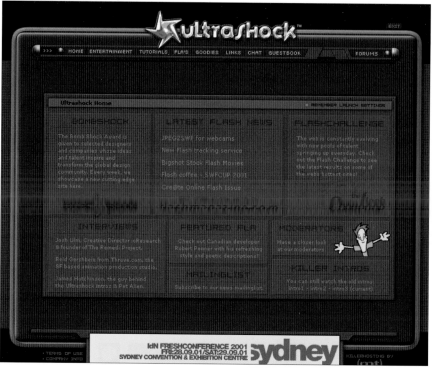

1 | 2
www.ultrashock.com is constructed using Flash, as befitting a resource site devoted to that particular technology. The menu bar and rollovers operate very smoothly, with transitions which would be hard to achieve in DHTML.

3
The Virtual World window at www.davidbowie.com uses subtle Flash rollovers that blend into the overall design.

stop playback, jump to a specified frame, or adjust the sound—and they can do things inside the movie. The element they are controlling must then be an instance of a movie-clip symbol. In this case, a script attached to a button and activated by an event may start or stop a movie clip playing, move its position on the stage, or change its color or opacity. An example of this is a remote rollover. A button symbol on the stage would have a script attached that activated when the mouse passed over. The script would instruct a movie-clip symbol to start playing, or to change its appearance, thus giving a remote rollover effect.

In order to provide smooth navigation through a site that is mainly HTML, scripts can use the Flash action getURL. This tells the browser to load a new page into a frame. So, by using a Flash menu consisting of buttons with getURL actions attached, we can provide animated controls such as rollovers without having to grapple directly with DHTML.

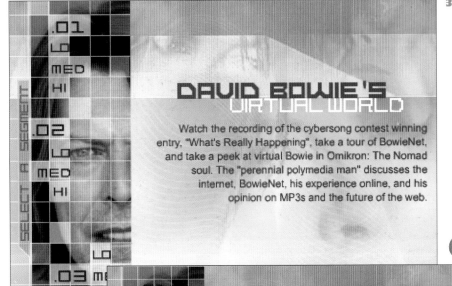

ADVANCED INTERACTIVITY IN FLASH

There are two ways in which Flash facilitates the design of advanced interactive animation. We can respond to mouse or keyboard events in unconventional ways, or we can extend the repertoire to include more advanced elements such as draggable movie clips, or the detection of collisions between movie clips.

A number of interactive showcase sites created by Flash designers and animators use scripts to track the path of the mouse as the user moves over the Flash movie. This is not just a sequence of mouse-over events; Flash can track the coordinates of the mouse in the movie window. The use of this data is up to the designer, of course, but it can be used to generate trails of multiple duplicate instances of animated or still clips, giving the impression that the mouse is painting with animated shapes, perhaps. Similarly, the script may use calculations to create other responses to the mouse tracks using the mouse's coordinates as variables in the calculation, which then generates or displays other animated elements, perhaps elsewhere on the screen. Flash has considerable potential for interactivity of this kind, but it requires a knowledge of ActionScript. It is possible to acquire and adapt scripts made available by other people, but beyond that there is no shortcut if we want to create some original interactive animation.

1
At the Flash site www.randommedia.co.uk visitors create an insect avatar in which they control mutation and randomize the generation of new insect options.

2
The "nodes with submenus" interactive menu structure at www.typospace.com/v3 offers a powerful, and what seems to be 3D, alternative to conventional interface elements.

Some Flash sites give their functional elements this treatment, for example, making an animated menu feature draggable. It is debatable whether this enhances the site, and a general rule is that it is not a good idea to exploit all Flash's potential for interactivity just because we know how to do it. It is fun to make things move around, but interactive elements should have a clear purpose, whether functional or aesthetic.

At www.typospace.com/v3 there is a demonstration of the potential for responding to mouse events in unusual ways. A simple graphic structure represents nodes with submenus. When a place name is clicked, a submenu that echoes the shape of the whole appears. If the name is pulled with the mouse the shape of the element to which it is attached appears to stretch toward the user in real-time, giving the 3D illusion. Dragging on any part of the background makes the whole structure revolve in the orientation of the mouse drag. The elements shrink and recede or grow, obeying the conventions of perspective. The rotations also speed up and slow down in response to the speed of the mouse, and the structure moves in accordance with the laws of physics. What is amazing is that Flash is not able to work with 3D; the whole thing is an illusion.

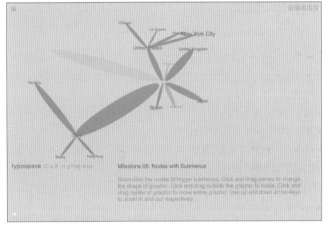

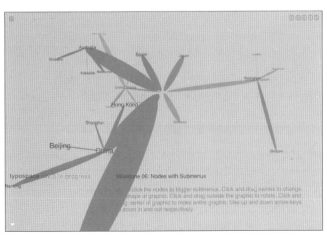

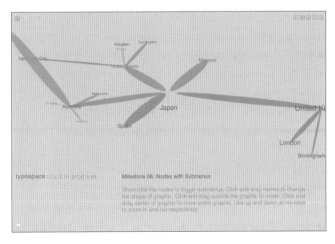

FLASH BY ANY OTHER NAME ...

LiveMotion Showcase

May, 2001

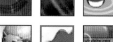

Yellow Duck Design
Yellow Duck Design created this animation to introduce the best finance site at the Webby Awards. The design team shot footage, edited it in Adobe Premiere® and Adobe After Effects®, and then imported it into LiveMotion.

☐ View the Flash movie

E-mail this story
to a friend

It is no longer necessary to use Flash to create SWF output for Web pages. Macromedia have published a specification of the format of SWF files. This means that programmers can write new software, or alter existing code, in order to generate SWFs. There are now several alternatives to Flash for creating SWF files: LiveMotion, Illustrator, and After Effects by Adobe, as well as Macromedia's Fireworks.

When LiveMotion was first released it was assumed to be Adobe's answer to Flash. Adobe have tried to shed this image but, in terms of functionality, it is certainly Flash's closest rival. Because it came onto the Web animation scene rather late it has not yet enjoyed widespread acceptance, but it does provide most of the features that Flash users expect. It uses a Timeline and object animation, in which objects can have many layers.

After Effects, which has long been respected as a high-end video post-production and motion graphics application, can now also export SWF format. The excellent facilities that After Effects offers make this an attractive option for producing superior Flash animation.

1 | 2
At www.adobe.com/web/gallery/lvmflipbook you can find many examples of the different ways in which other software applications can be used to create SWF output for Web sites.

3
Craig Drake was commissioned by Adobe to create this splash animation with LiveMotion.

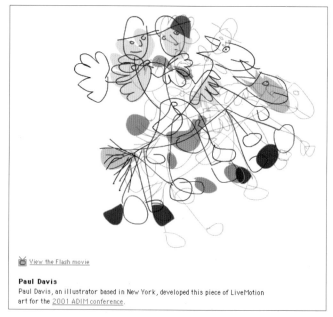

☐ View the Flash movie

Paul Davis
Paul Davis, an illustrator based in New York, developed this piece of LiveMotion art for the 2001 ADIM conference.

It is also a good way of producing Flash work that has its origins in video footage. After Effects does not provide scripting support, with the exception that it is possible to attach a getURL action to the SWF.

Illustrator is a standard vector graphics application. It can create an animated sequence by exporting the layers of an Illustrator document to the frames of an SWF, in the order in which they are stacked. The frame rate for such an animation is set in the export dialog box. This process can create Flash graphic symbols out of the vector objects in the Illustrator document, which helps to optimize the file, and can be useful if that SWF is imported into Flash for further work. This might happen frequently since Illustrator offers no scripting facilities.

Fireworks is Macromedia's Web graphics application, designed as an adjunct to Dreamweaver. Like Adobe's ImageReady it can create animations, and has onion skinning and tweening facilities. Like Illustrator, it has no support for scripting, and so actions have to be attached elsewhere.

Although widely used, Flash is not a Web standard in the official sense. The W3C has been supporting the development of a new format, SVG (Scalable Vector Graphics), not yet ratified. Animation is supported in SVG through a language acceptable to Web browsers—JavaScript, for example. Because there are no software packages available to make this job easier for designers, it looks as though SVG will be outflanked by Flash for some time.

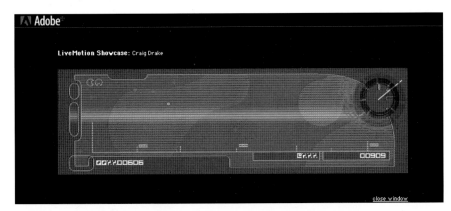

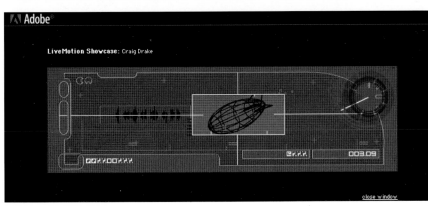

INTRODUCING SHOCKWAVE

In the days when multimedia could only be distributed on CD-ROMs, much multimedia content was created in Macromedia Director, considered the industry standard. Multimedia CD-ROMs did not enjoy much success, however, while the Internet developed rapidly. Macromedia therefore created a new delivery format called Shockwave for export from Director, specifically for use on the World Wide Web.

Only Director can export Shockwave movies, which require a browser plug-in called Shockwave Player. Macromedia estimate that over 200 million users have downloaded this plug-in (which also includes Flash Player), so a very large number of people can access Shockwave material on the Web. For Web animation designers, however, the picture is not so rosy. Many will find that it is very difficult to become competent in the use of Director for Web content creation, but it is very powerful.

Shockwave is a rich media format, because Director can work with almost any media type: all the still image formats; animated GIFs; all the usual sound formats including MP3 audio; Flash movies; QuickTime and AVI files; text in various formats; other Director movies; and even PowerPoint files. Recently, Macromedia have added support for 3D formats, making Shockwave by far the most versatile delivery format for Web animation.

Director does provide some basic tools for creating vector and bitmapped graphics, and text elements. Most designers, however, prefer to create these in other applications and import them into Director for assembly, animation, and the addition of scripts and interactive controls. Animation facilities similar to those in Flash are available, including tweening. Like Flash, Director uses a timeline—called the score—with key frames and multiple layers. Director differs from Flash in some ways, however. In Director the media elements, or cast

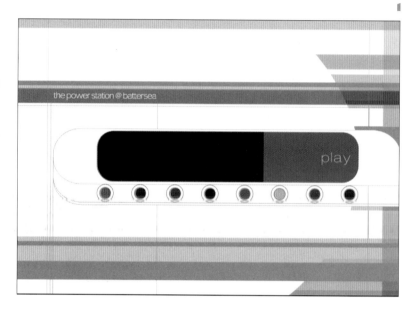

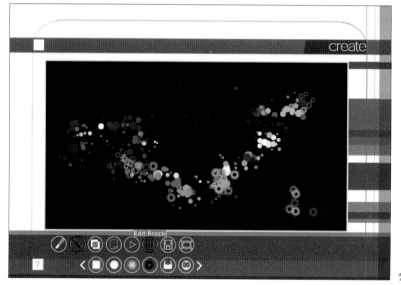

members, to be used in the project (confusingly called the movie, as in Flash) are not placed directly on the stage, but are represented on the stage by "sprites."

When preparing Shockwave movies for the Internet, careful planning is required. The right parts of the movie must be available to the user when they are needed. Shockwave is a streaming technology—it does not all download before the movie starts playing at the user's end. When a Shockwave movie is first accessed, the media elements (cast members) that are required for the first frame—or for the first few frames if specified by the designer—will download, and then the movie will start. After this the downloading will continue in the background—according to the order specified in the Director score—while the movie progresses. If the work is interactive it is therefore necessary to anticipate what user input might occur at any point, and to ensure that the necessary cast members have

been downloaded by that point, so that playback continues without delay. However, for straightforward animation design, many designers find Flash more accessible than Director, and so there are many more Web sites animated by Flash than by Shockwave. But for more complex and media-rich work—especially now that Director supports 3D formats—Shockwave is undoubtedly superior.

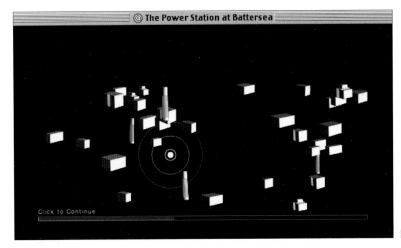

3

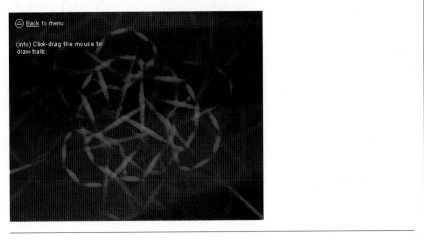

1 | 2
The Shockwave Web site devoted to the regeneration of London's Battersea Power Station— www.thepowerstation. co.uk—has a wide range of interactive features from Shockwave menus to a mini drawing application, and exploits Shockwave's potential for rich media presentations.

3
The original trailer for the Battersea Power Station site was also made in Shockwave, and includes an elaborate loading sequence.

4
The interactive collection of "Bits and Pieces" by Daniel Brown, exhibited at www.noodlebox.com, are all created in Shockwave. In this piece the user's mouse movements are tracked and used to generate patterns of light trails.

4

INTERACTIVE SHOCKWAVE

Director comes with a scripting language called Lingo, which enables interactivity and other programmable behavior in Shockwave. This predates Flash ActionScript, and is more powerful although broadly similar. However, Lingo is a different language, so designers working with material in both Flash and Shockwave will need to be multilingual.

Although hand-coded scripts can be written in Lingo to enable a wide range of custom actions, it does come with many pre-packaged bits of scripts—called behaviors—which are ready to use and therefore require no scripting knowledge. These are provided in a set of libraries, which include behavior categories such as Animation, Controls, Internet, Media, Navigation, and Text. Thus we can use many scripts to control animation and interactivity without knowing how to write them ourselves. It is also possible, for those who understand something about Lingo, to customize the included behaviors to make them more original or appropriate. Those designers able to write fluently in Lingo may program sophisticated interactivity and animation; particle animation could be created in this way, for example. Shockwave is used for the more demanding online games since its combination of rich media formats with powerful scripting make it suited to the demands of users who expect high-quality graphics and animation combined with elaborate interactivity.

Shockwave may be used for functional interactive Web page elements as well as for fun and for interactive artworks. Tomato use an elaborate Shockwave navigation feature at their Web site www.tomato.co.uk. There are four main menu items, which appear as text over a background graphic when the page is accessed. Before mouse-over the whole thing is static, but with the mouse-over any part of the navigation window there is movement of various kinds. The menu items and the background graphic both move, in different ways, as do the submenus. All the animation in this lively navigation occurs in response to user-initiated events—its normal state on the page is still.

1

The Shockwave menu at www.tomato.co.uk challenges interface design conventions. Shockwave allows tomato to create a Web page in keeping with their other design work.

2

www.kha-music.com— Ici la lune's Web site for the French funk-rock group Khâ,— features a Shockwave presentation in which even the loading sequence is interactive.

2

Shockwave enables designers to break down interface conventions, and create Web pages that reflect a specific style. It is the best tool for this because it uses many kinds of media. However, unconventional interfaces may raise issues of usability, and a navigation or menu design that leaves users guessing is only appropriate where their interest is sustained. For sites that need clear functionality to provide impatient viewers with rapid responses, less elaborate animation is preferable.

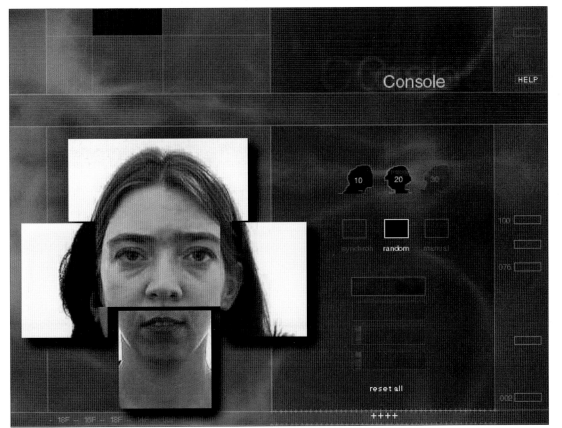

3

The shockwave version of digital medialab at testphase.at/medialab features a sophisticated custom interface that allows users to control experiments with bitmapped material.

3

SHOCKWAVE AND 3D

When thinking about 3D it is essential to remember that what we see on the screen is, of necessity, not 3D. The graphic representation is always 2D—it cannot be anything else. However, there is a vital distinction in Web and other computer design between a 2D illusion of 3D that has been created in a 2D application or by nondigital means, and those 2D screen images that are output from a 3D application.

Various technologies, including pen and paper or paint and canvas, provide us with 2D illusions of 3D; this gave rise to the conventions of perspective. On the Web, these illusions could be presented in animated form in Flash, animated GIFs, or a video format such as QuickTime. Most films and videos are concerned entirely with presenting 2D pictures of a 3D world. Some advanced Flash animation can produce very convincing representations of 3D, with models that can apparently be fully manipulated in a 3D space.

How is this different from genuine 3D? With processes this advanced the distinction is becoming blurred; all 3D graphics are created in this way. However, in "genuine" 3D applications the generation of the 2D projections is built-in and does not require scripting. Also, the models and algorithms for rendering are more sophisticated. They include calculations to take account of textures, reflections, and different sorts of light sources, as well as their interaction with the surfaces of the models. It should be noted that Flash can only perform calculations and present 2D graphic responses—it cannot import or work with 3D models from 3D applications.

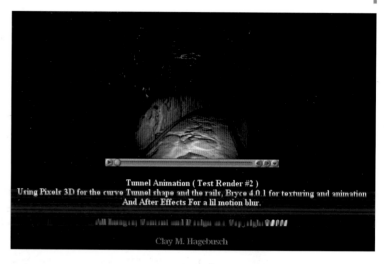

Tunnel Animation (Test Render #2)
Using Pixels 3D for the curve Tunnel shape and the rails, Bryce 4.0.1 for texturing and animation
And After Effects For a lil motion blur.

Clay M. Hagebusch

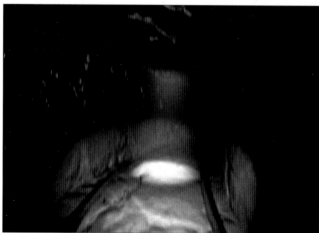

Clay M. Hagebusch created this animated ride through a tunnel in dedicated 3D modeling applications, and saved the result as a QuickTime movie. When we view this at www.phase2.net/claygraphics we are therefore looking at a 2D record of navigation through a genuine 3D environment.

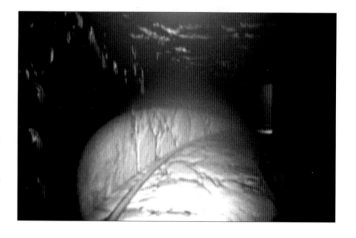

Working with 3D animation on the Web is not easy, and until recently it has not really been possible. 3D applications use mathematics to describe objects geometrically, and, in conjunction with bitmaps and other elements, to specify surface properties, lighting, and textures. For genuine 3D animation to work over the Internet, the 3D model with all its information has to be sent down the wires and rendered in real-time on the client machine. This is a tough job: it requires hardware acceleration and software on the user's computer that can handle the 3D model. New computers may now have 3D graphics accelerators built in, and there will be some software present in the Operating System (for example, OpenGL) for dealing with 3D, but many domestic users may have older machines that cannot cope, unless they are avid games players.

3D Web animation involves large amounts of data, so bandwidth can be a problem. However, new technologies have been developed to work around these problems. Foremost among these is Shockwave 3D, which is built in to the latest version of Macromedia's Director Shockwave Studio. This incorporates an automatic process by which resolution can be adjusted to suit the bandwidth of the user, and other conditions. The designer simply creates a high resolution model and provides some hints, in the form of parameters, which state what can be omitted if necessary. Thus, viewers with lower bandwidth will see a lower-quality version of the 3D animation—but at least they will see it. This adaptability not only allows adjustment for bandwidth and the viewer's processor, but makes other clever data-saving alterations, such as dropping the resolution as a 3D object gets further away from the camera. There are also alternative rendering options in Shockwave to suit different types of work: photo-realistic, engravings, or toons.

2

2
Robohunter 2: Spy City is an online game by Lego created in Shockwave 3D. At mindstorms.lego.com, players drive a robot vehicle through a virtual city environment using keyboard navigational controls. This is genuine Web 3D because the 3D model itself is available to the user, rather than just a 2D record of it.

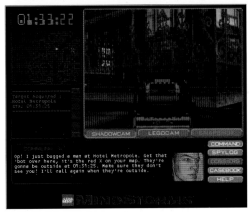

VIRTUAL WORLDS

The term Virtual Reality (VR) originally referred to an immersive experience that involved wearing special equipment, such as a helmet or a glove, to assist in the illusion that we were actually present in a different environment. VR is still used in that sense, but on the Web it does not yet have that meaning; such advanced technology exists only in science fiction. However, there is an increasing amount of VR material on the Web, and it is, by definition, animated or, more correctly, capable of animation by the viewer.

All VR is interactive; this is what distinguishes it from a 3D model or scene. A VR environment is one through which we can navigate in 3D, as though we were in a real space. A VR object is one which we can manipulate in 3D, as though it were real.

There are three established VR technologies for the Web— QuickTime VR (QTVR), VRML, and

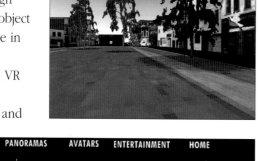

Java 3D. Newer technologies, such as Viewpoint Metastream, have emerged recently. It should be noted that all VR technologies, with the exception of Java 3D, require browser plug-ins.

QTVR is not a fully-fledged VR technology. The illusion of a three-dimensional space or object is achieved simply by taking—or creating—a series of still images around a 360° panorama, either by rotating the camera tripod or by rotating the object itself, and including views above and below. These are stitched together in a specified way and exported as QTVR, which includes standard controls for viewing. It is possible to look left, right, up and down, and to zoom in and out. However, the fake nature of the method is revealed on zooming in, as the image typically becomes increasingly pixellated. The supposed zoom is just magnifying that section of the image.

Planet 9 specialize in 3D and VRML. Their VirtualSOMA (South of Market area in San Francisco) was the first ever virtual city on the Internet, back in 1995. Since then it has been improved and enhanced in line with newer versions of VRML. After more than a million downloads, it is still online at www.planet9.com.

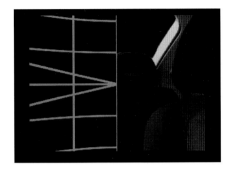

2
At www.beetle.de viewers can look all around the inside of a virtual car, courtesy of QuickTime VR. The Star Trek holodeck appearance during download shows how the 2D panorama is wrapped around 360°, with the viewer in the center.

VRML is more sophisticated. It is a scene description language and, like HTML, it can be hand-coded. Complete 3D scenes can be described in code, without the use of any kind of graphics application. However, few designers would choose this route. VRML is automatically generated complete from some 3D applications, but if we do not have a suitable application for this job it is possible just to construct the 3D models in a standard 3D program and then assemble them by writing some fairly simple VRML code. Its limitations are apparent when viewing any VRML scene on the Web— it hardly compares favorably with the quality we have come to expect from computer-generated 3D scenes in films, for example. However, it should be noted that, unusually for Web animation formats, there is not just one standard plug-in for viewing VRML as there is for proprietary formats such as Flash and Shockwave. In fact, there is a plethora of alternative plug-ins for viewing VRML, each of which offers different levels of quality, interfaces, and navigational controls. For this reason it is particularly difficult to anticipate what the viewer will see when they access a VRML element. This problem does not arise with Java 3D, because the controls are custom-built into the Java applet that runs on the viewer's computer.

3
QTVR allows the viewer to zoom in— but the pixellation typical of extreme QTVR zooms reveals that in fact the 2D image is just being blown up.

WEB VIDEO

The fundamental problem with video is that it is big—it involves larger file sizes than any other format for animation. As a result, the many viewers without broadband access are likely to find video presentations frustrating or disappointing. Frustrating if they have to wait ten minutes before they can view anything; disappointing if the video is streamed and keeps starting and stopping, with sound failing to synchronize with the picture, or if the picture is of poor quality as a result of excessive compression.

The concept of Web video is somewhat anomalous, because video's origins lie in magnetic tape, and the need to record and play back live-action sequences. In the context of other Web technologies that support moving images, it is no longer clear what video is. Perhaps the most helpful working definition is that Web video is based on specific architectures, primarily QuickTime, RealVideo (usually known just as Real), and Windows Media. Each requires the presence of plug-ins

1

QuickTime clips of tomato's work can be viewed embedded in the page at www.tomato.co.uk. A range of good-quality options is available for different bandwidths and versions of the plug-in.

2

Dr. Mark J. Carlotto created the "Face on Mars" animations from genuine Viking orbiter data. They play well as compressed QuickTime movies embedded in his Web page at www.psrw.com/~markc/MediaProducts/Animations.

The Face on Mars

The Fortress

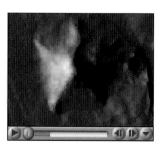

The D & M Pyramid

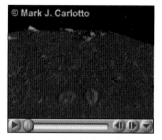

Cydonia Animation

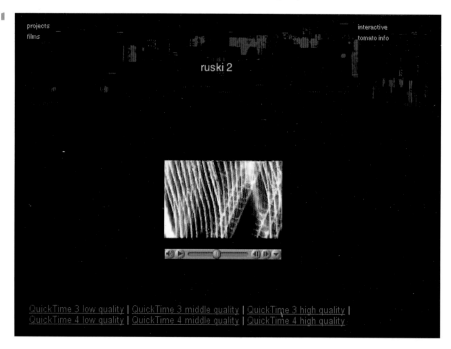

for video playback. Most Internet users will have at least one of these plug-ins, but few will have them all. It is best to avoid video formats unless there is really no other choice.

Video is still the primary way of displaying long sequences of bitmapped images. However, Flash also handles bitmaps and is becoming a viable alternative. Because video always involves large file sizes, material intended for Web distribution in any video format will often have to be substantially compressed, with a consequent loss of quality. Another common stratagem for reducing file size is to reduce the physical dimensions, in other words, the window size. This typically should be no more than 320 by 240 pixels to be suitable for low-bandwidth access. To go from almost full screen size at 72 dpi to this reduced size at the same resolution means discarding a lot of information. If video clips are intended to be fully downloaded before they start playing—as with QuickTime movies—they will also have to be kept short if the viewer is not to lose patience.

When video is streamed, the length of the clip is much less important and data transfer rate is the overriding factor because this determines whether the information

reaches the viewer fast enough for convincing playback. Since most ordinary modems receive data at a maximum rate of 56 kbps, and often slower, the data rate of video needs to be kept very low.

Despite the problems associated with Web video, it is used widely. For animation, it is primarily used where the original material was not made for the Web. In this case it is usually still the best option for dissemination over the Internet, but in order to maintain picture quality high download times must continue for the time being.

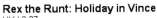

3

3
At www.atomfilms.com viewers are offered a choice of video formats in which to view episodes of Aardman's well-known animations.

4
Web video is still problematic. This is not an experimental abstract work, but a streamed character animation that has been rendered unrecognizable by technological problems.

4

SPECIALIZED ANIMATION TOOLS

There are some specialized, low-cost applications that provide effective facilities for original animation on desktop platforms. These include Corel Painter, Corel Bryce, and Curious Labs Poser—all of which were at one time a part of the Metacreations software stable.

Painter is known for its realistic natural media tools. It enables computer-based artists to create work in simulated oils or watercolor, and so on, and it provides simulated supports in the form of textured backgrounds, such as canvas. Painter offers a wide range of customizable brushes and a number of special effects, plus an almost unrivaled facility for creating large-scale animations in the form of a framestack. When used in conjunction with a pressure-sensitive pen on a graphics tablet, it is capable of more detailed and subtle work than any other desktop application, and makes Photoshop's painting tools look positively primitive.

Poser and Bryce are effective low-end 3D applications, and both have acquired cult followings. Poser is devoted to creating and animating 3D figures, and Bryce is concerned with modeling and animating landscapes and scenery, although it has been expanded to handle other 3D objects.

Poser is surprisingly easy to use, and comes with a library of figures, clothing, and so on, which can be adapted as needed. The animation facilities are straightforward and animations can be previewed in the application itself. Although inexpensive, it supports some sophisticated features such as inverse kinematics and ray tracing, and its models may be exported for use in other 3D applications. Poser animation may be saved in a number of formats, including animated GIFs or video formats for use on Web sites. Even very small Poser figures, presented in an animated GIF on an otherwise static page, for example, at www.the-forge.ie, can provide startlingly effective animation.

Bryce is famous for its unconventional interface designed by Kai Krause, and its uniqueness does not stop there. Originally designed for creating still images from custom-designed landscapes, Bryce was expanded

1
The Forge Studios Ltd. create and supply Poser animations. The graphics for their Web site at www.the-forge.ie were created by a multistage process using Painter, Poser, and Bryce.

2
The landscapes and tunnel are modeled in Bryce.

to support animation and 3D objects. It is capable of high-resolution results, and provides extensive modeling controls for experienced designers. Multiple lights and cameras may be animated, and ray tracing can be adjusted to suit the desired output resolution.

Unfortunately, 3D Web animation has not yet sufficiently matured for Bryce to be fully exploited, and most current Bryce animation is presented in video format. With increasing bandwidth, and the development of 3D animation support for the Web, Bryce animation will soon be more widely seen.

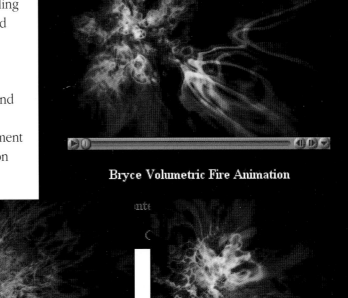

Bryce Volumetric Fire Animation

4
The figures are created in Poser, and the whole is combined to play as an animated GIF embedded in the Web page, in which the figures constantly emerge from the tiny tunnel and run into the swirling light effect in the larger one.

3
Clay M. Hagebusch uses Bryce to create impressive animations that are embedded as QuickTime movies on Web pages at www.phase2.net/ claygraphics.

4

5
Painter is used to add new colors, textures, and detail for the tunnel animation.

5

ONCE UPON A FOREST

Www.once-upon-a-forest.com is one of Flashmaster Joshua Davis' award-winning Web sites, based on the premise that it is more rewarding to explore than to reach conclusions. Deliberately enigmatic, it challenges the conventions of Web site design, and provides no answers or user support—just a rich tapestry of sound and animation that grows from month to month.

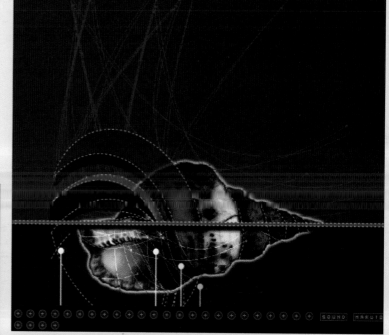

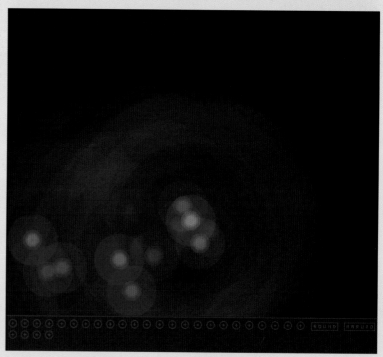

PRAYSTATION

Another well-known site by Joshua Davis, www.praystation.com acts as a sounding board, personal record, and exhibition space for cutting-edge Flash design and experimentation. With Flash scripts being made available on an open source basis, designers can take advantage of each other's achievements and innovations, as in the example here using species-B by James Paterson of Presstube.

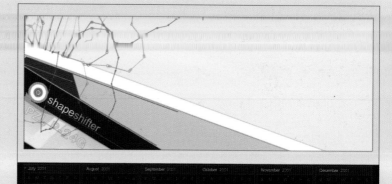

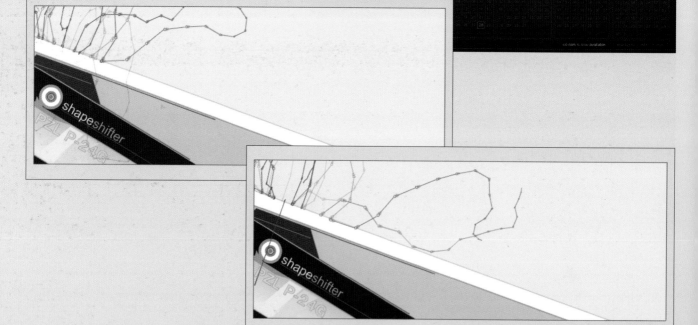

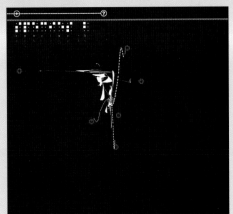
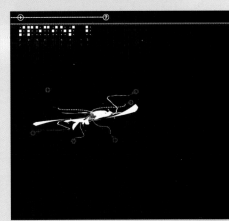

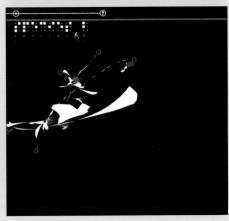
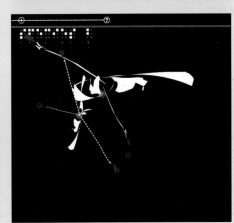

BELGRADE 2001

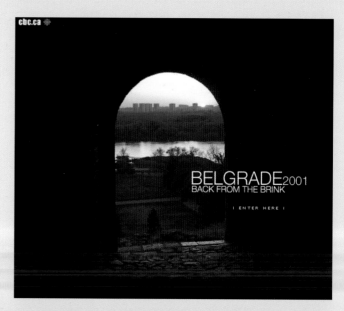

The Belgrade 2001 Web site was developed by Rob McLaughlin and a team of Canadian Broadcasting Company Radio 3 producers, who spent ten days in Belgrade making still, audio, and video recordings of this devastated city entitled "Back from the Brink." The Web site, which can be found at cbc.ca/onair/shows/belgrade2001, makes original and interesting use of Flash and Fireworks to present a moving photographic essay in which focused images resolve from fragments, and texts and sounds are interwoven into an extensive documentary tapestry.

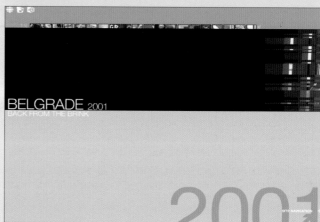

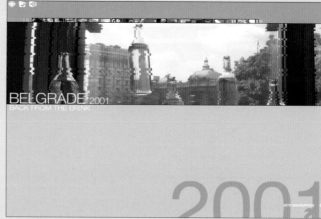

BELGRADE 2001
THE INTERNET REVOLUTION?

The telecommunications infrastructure may be crumbling and most people may be too poor to afford a computer, but through a decade of war the internet was a lifeline to the outside world.

Virtual communities grew not because technology made them possible, but out of necessity. There probably was no "internet revolution" in Serbia. Revolutions are fought by people not computers. But without the Net, life — and art — would have been much more isolated.

// THE INTERNET REVOLUTION?
In the Western press, the popular uprising in Serbia was dubbed the "Internet Revolution". But how much of a role did it really have in toppling the regime of Slobodan Milosevic? Chris Boyce from DNTO reports.
➤ CLICK TO LISTEN TO REPORT

// WAR FRAMES // ZORAN NASKOVSKI
From the Center for Contemporary Art's exposition during war time, this Web project documents television's reality, capturing frames of programming during air raids during NATO bombings."
➤ CLICK FOR PROJECT

// HOUSE OF IMAGES // JOVAN CEKIC
"Each house has photos to show all around and present in public, but also has a lot of hidden, those which people in the house are ashamed of and do not want even to remember... which one can accidentally find."
➤ CLICK FOR PROJECT

// THE IKEDA ATTRACTOR // SMILJANA PESIC
One of the many projects found at Cyberrex, the portal to urban belgrade culture that grew out of the need to move online after the government closed the theatre and tried to confiscate their equipment.
➤ CLICK FOR PROJECT

101

BELGRADE 2001
BACK FROM THE BRINK

2001

BELGRADE 2001
BACK FROM THE BRINK

For the last 10 years of his rule, Milosevic...

The former president removed, disabled and ruthlessly persecuted independent...

It is estimated that in the last decade, 400,000 left the country. One certain political fact, economically destroyed, politically driven.

Many of those who chose to stay were as both endured and resisted a regime and a...

They created art that challenged, defied a nation towards change.

They continue to create art that depicts, hopefully to a future free of turmoil and so...

These are their stories.

2001

BELGRADE 2001

BELGRADE 2001

BELGRADE 2001

BELGRADE 2001

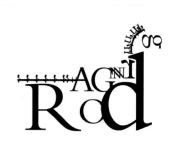

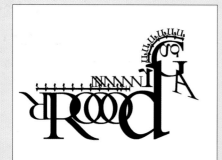

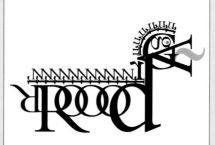

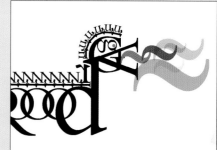

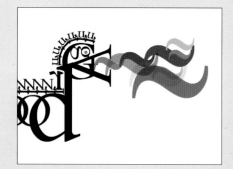

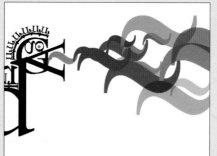

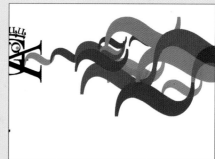

BEMBO'S ZOO

This delightful and original Flash site, created by graphic designer Roberto de Vicq de Cumptich, is created in connection with his children's ABC picturebook of the same title. He has animated the site to do things with the Bembo typeface that few typographers or animators can have dreamed of. The Web site, which can be found at www.bemboszoo.com, also uses sound to support an elegant and unique work in motion graphics.

Bembo's ZOO

Click here if you have Flash

Click here if you don't have Flash

" This high-concept abecedary, the picture book debut for deVicq de Cumptich, should delight collectors of stylish picture books and aficionados of the graphic arts."
— *Publishers Weekly*

" In this first book for children, de Cumptich.... has created an abecedary of animals made entirely from Bembo letterforms and punctuations marks-nothing else. And you know the concept works."
— *New York Times*

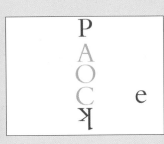

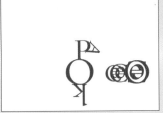

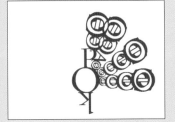

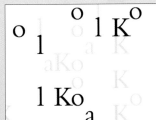

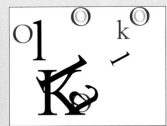

SWITCHEROOZOO AND FLASHCAN

The Web sites www.switcheroozoo.com and www.flashcan.com offer interactive Flash fun and creativity for children of all ages. At Switcheroozoo, visitors can selectively morph parts of an animal's body to create an entirely new creature, while learning a few interesting animal facts as they go along. Flashcan presents a set of Flash e-card templates, previously created by designers and illustrators, for users to create their own animated cards to send. Scaling, rotation, duplication, and transparency allow for many permutations of the basic elements.

104

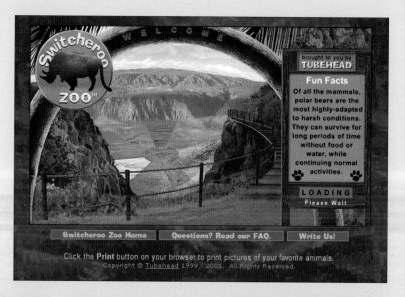

flashcan

They design it, you mess with it. That's the idea behind Flashcan. Your creations can be edited, saved, sent, and printed. Flashcan was created by the fine folks at zinc Roe design. Have a use for Flashcan? We now offer hosted licensing packages.

the designs

We have some great new designs for your flashcan pleasure. Big thanks to all our contributors. If you would like to contribute artwork drop us an email at: flashcan@zincroe.com.

the gallery

Keep them coming in! We will soon be opening a little gallery of some of the best flashcan creations. Email your flashcan creations to gallery@flashcan.com.

flashcan on Family.ca

The Family Channel has adopted flashcan for their card swap egreetings. Together we will be rolling out a series of fun card designs over the coming months. Take a look!

Flashcan ©2001 zinc Roe design
www.zincroe.com

WILD BRAIN, INC.

Founded in 1994, Wild Brain, Inc. has produced an unprecedented library of 232 award-winning episodes of Web animations based on 36 original ideas and 6 classic cartoon characters from the Hanna-Barbera library. Wild Brain's Web animation has been lauded in, amongst others, Fortune, Business Week, TV Guide, and Rolling Stone magazines, and has been distributed by both international and domestic partners including Yahoo!, Sony, and Cartoon Network. These stylish webisodes at www.wildbrain.com rely primarily on Flash as a delivery format.

wildbrain.com™

WATCH THIS SHOW!

Episode 1	Episode 2
Episode 3	Episode 4
Episode 5	Episode 6
Episode 7	Episode 8
Episode 9	Episode 10
Episode 11	Episode 12

"A square-jawed cubist PI blasts his way through a black-and-white cityscape in stylish neo-noir escapades." -- *Editors of Yahoo! Internet Life Magazine*

1st Place Internet Action/Adventure at the World Animation Celebration

Credits

Directed by
Rogue Ball

JOE PARADISE
Get lost in the world of JOE PARADISE, create BALLESTEROS, where JOE tries to escape his and disappear somewhere in SOME CITY, som 9 to 5.

For information on exhibiting these shows on te or another Web site, please email distribution@

© 2001 wildbrain.com, Inc. All Rights Reserved

SERIEs

News

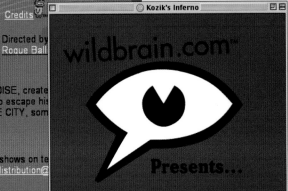

wildbrain.com™

Presents...

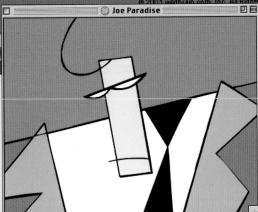

@ Joe Paradise

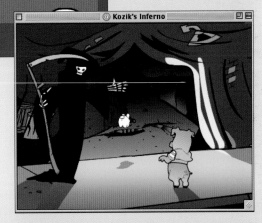

@ Kozik's Inferno

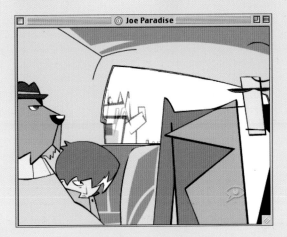

@ Joe Paradise

@ Kozik's Inferno

SONY: THE STATION

Sony Online Entertainment provide a wide range of high-quality online games at station.sony.com, from simple puzzles to the massively multiplayer EverQuest, which typically supports tens of thousands of players online at any one time. Flash trailers for Star Wars Galaxies demonstrate the sophistication of this latest addition to online game playing.

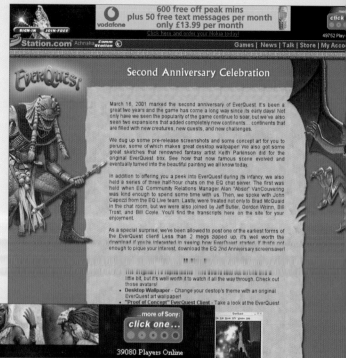

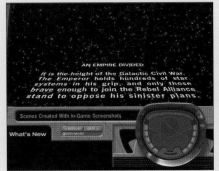

LEGO

The Web site showcase for the ever-popular children's toy Lego offers a bright and lively animated interface, as well as a range of interactive Flash activities, which include animations and games featuring animated adaptations of the Lego models. Children of all ages are catered for at www.lego.com.

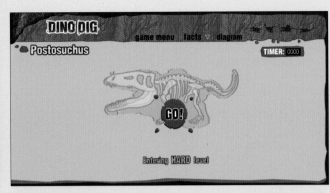

DINO DIG   game menu   facts ▽   diagram   TIMER: 0000
Postosuchus
GO!
Entering HARD level

DINO DIG   game menu   facts ▽   diagram   TIMER: 0000
Postosuchus

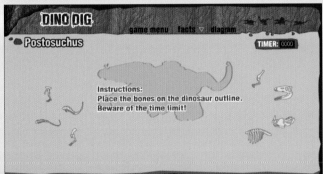

DINO DIG   game menu   facts ▽   diagram   TIMER: 0000
Postosuchus
Instructions:
Place the bones on the dinosaur outline.
Beware of the time limit!

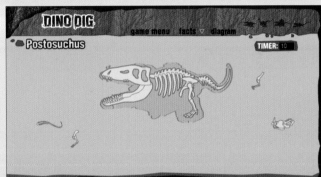

DINO DIG   game menu   facts ▽   diagram   TIMER: 10
Postosuchus

DINO DIG   game menu   facts ▽   diagram   TIMER: 0000
Postosuchus

DINO DIG   game menu   facts ▽   diagram   TIMER: 0000
Postosuchus

PLANET 9 STUDIOS

Planet 9 Studios specialize in the creation of 3D and virtual reality worlds so it is no surprise that their Web site offers examples of the very best virtual reality on the Web. Their online VRML environments at www.planet9.com allow the visitor to experience the latest advances in the use of this technology.

VRML Panorama From the Pacific Crest Trail Near the Back Side of Alpine Meadows at Lake Tahoe in California June•1996

If the image above is fuzzy or seamed, you need a new VRML plug-in. Please go to our tools page.
For more information Planet 9 Studios can be reached at archive@planet9.com

Contents Copyright © Planet 9 Studios, 1996

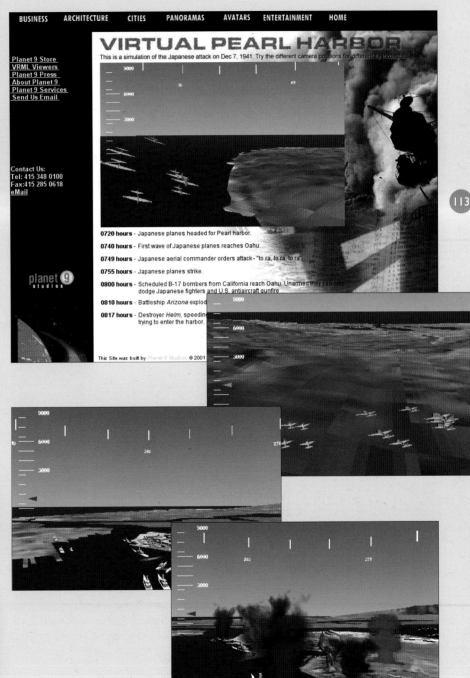

BUSINESS   ARCHITECTURE   CITIES   PANORAMAS   AVATARS   ENTERTAINMENT   HOME

Planet 9 Store
VRML Viewers
Planet 9 Press
About Planet 9
Planet 9 Services
Send Us Email

Contact Us:
Tel: 415 348 0100
Fax: 415 285 0618
eMail

planet 9
studios

VIRTUAL PEARL HARBOR

This is a simulation of the Japanese attack on Dec 7, 1941. Try the different camera positions for different fly-throughs.

0720 hours - Japanese planes headed for Pearl harbor.

0740 hours - First wave of Japanese planes reaches Oahu.

0749 hours - Japanese aerial commander orders attack - "to ra, to ra, to ra"

0755 hours - Japanese planes strike.

0800 hours - Scheduled B-17 bombers from California reach Oahu. Unarmed they can only dodge Japanese fighters and U.S. antiaircraft gunfire.

0810 hours - Battleship *Arizona* explodes

0817 hours - Destroyer *Helm*, speeding trying to enter the harbor.

This Site was built by Planet 9 Studios © 2001

113

NOODLEBOX: BITS AND PIECES

Bits and Pieces at www.noodlebox.com is an
interactive Shockwave site by Daniel Brown. The
visitor can create some beautiful effects by simply
dragging the mouse cursor across the screen. The feel
of the site is ethereal and it offers animation of a
delicacy not often seen elsewhere on the Web.

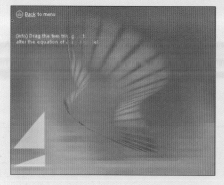

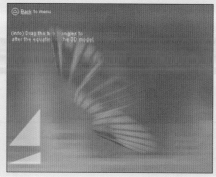

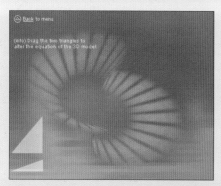

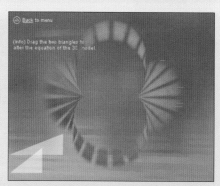

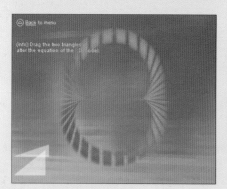

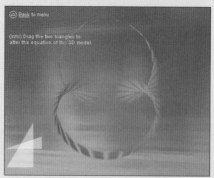

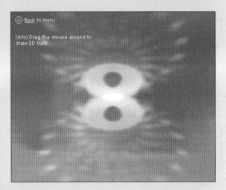

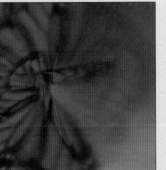

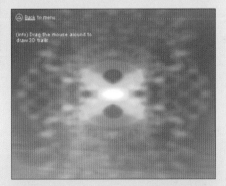

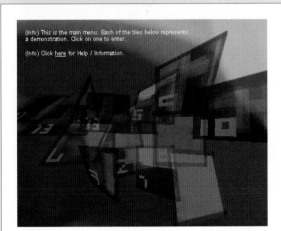

Bits and Pieces

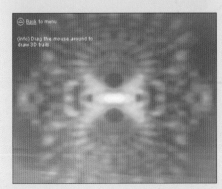

ICI LA LUNE

Based in Paris, Ici la Lune specialize in producing interactive Web sites with unusual navigation and rich media content. Their own site at www.icilalune.com, and the www.kha-music.com site, which they designed for a French funk-rock band, demonstrate some aspects of their ingenuity and originality.

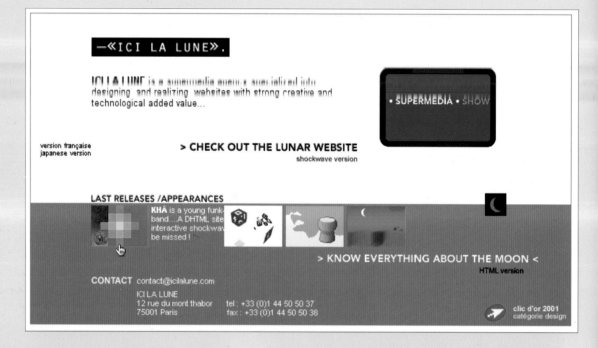

117

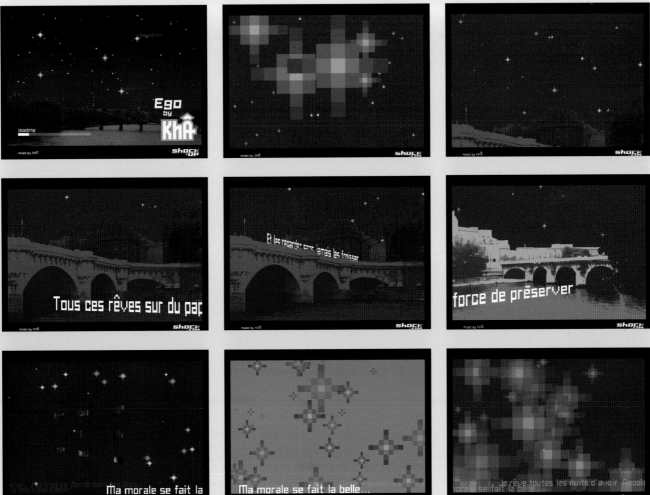

NESCAFÉ

At www.nescafe.co.uk and Nescafé's other inter-related Web sites, the pages are brought alive by the use of animated GIFs derived from Nescafé's global "Open Up" commercials. These touches of life in close-up, on the otherwise static and factual pages, give the site an added dimension and impact.

Coffee World

Origins
Ever wondered where coffee originally came from? A long, long time ago, in a land far away...

Tree to cup
How do you get that perfect cup of Nescafé? From tree to cup, follow the Nescafé trail.

Nutrition & health
Ever wondered how many calories or how much caffeine is in your cup of Nescafé? Find out here.

Did you know?
Discover fascinating facts about our senses of taste and aroma.

About Nescafé

"Open Up"

One thing, the world over, helps people to take time out, to listen to each other and to open up - a cup of coffee.

"Open Up" is our global campaign for Nescafé to celebrate the part that coffee plays in people's lives.

About Nescafé

"Open Up"

One thing, the world over, helps people to take time out, to listen to each other and to open up - a cup of coffee.

"Open Up" is our global campaign for Nescafé to celebrate the part that coffee plays in people's lives.

About Nescafé

"Open Up"

One thing, the world over, helps people to take time out, to listen to each other and to open up - a cup of coffee.

"Open Up" is our global campaign for Nescafé to celebrate the part that coffee plays in people's lives.

About Nescafé

"Open Up"

One thing, the world over, helps people to take time out, to listen to each other and to open up - a cup of coffee.

"Open Up" is our global campaign for Nescafé to celebrate the part that coffee plays in people's lives.

THE ART OF THE ANIMATED GIF

Animated GIFs are often associated with banner ads and other basic Web animation. But the animated GIF is a versatile format, capable of much more, and is easily incorporated into any Web page. Below is shown an animation by Marc Wielogroch, which is on display in the Internet Movie Machine at www.16color.com; right is one of Nescafé's animated GIFs embedded in a page at www.nescafe.com; and far right, the illustration and animation skills on www.jpgaultier.fr are shown off in an animated GIF.

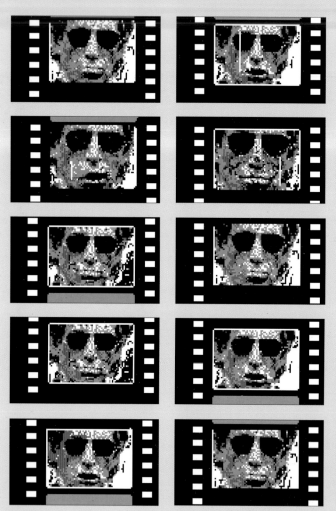

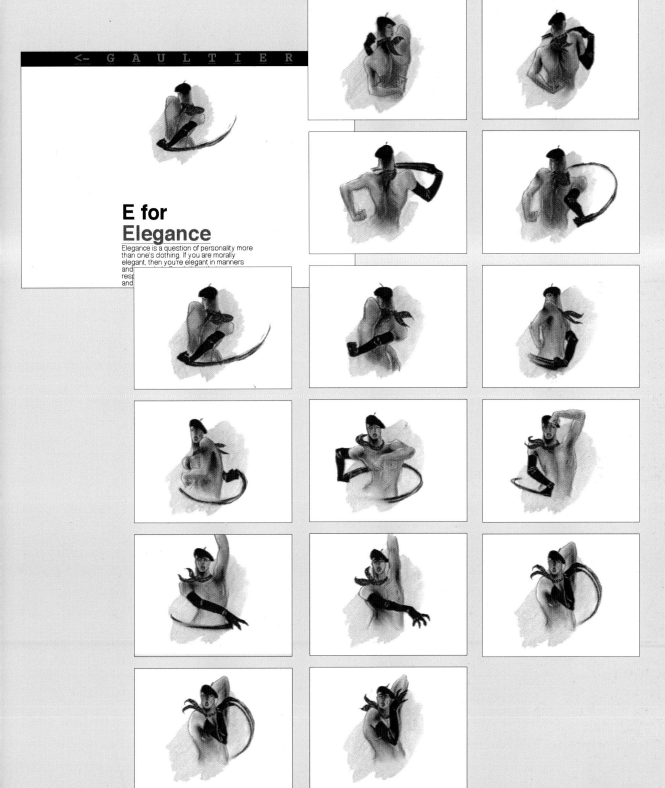

E for
Elegance

Elegance is a question of personality more than one's clothing. If you are morally elegant, then you're elegant in manners and
resp
and

JEAN-PAUL GAULTIER

The Web site celebrating the work of the famous French fashion designer Jean-Paul Gaultier is as charming and original as his own designs. At www.jpgaultier.fr a combined range of different animation technologies is used to create a site that is exciting, different, and très animé.

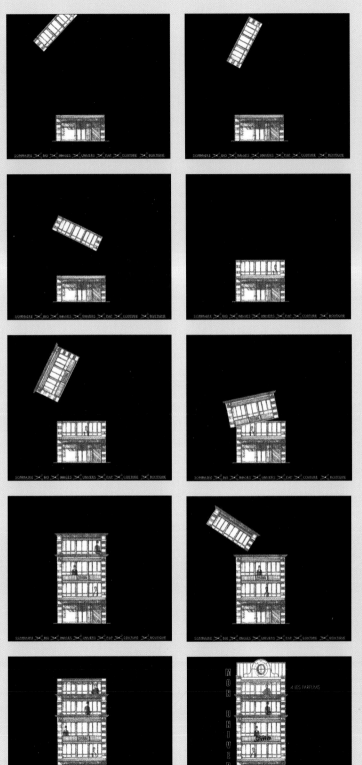

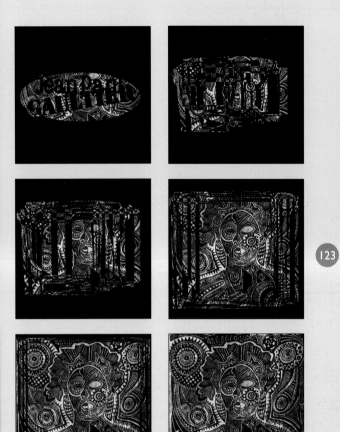

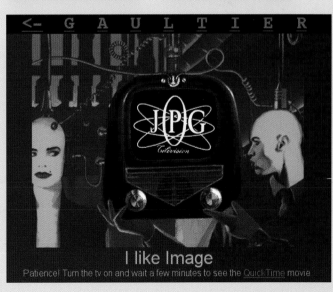

I like Image

Patience! Turn the tv on and wait a few minutes to see the QuickTime movie.

RANDOM MEDIA

The evolving Flash site www.randommedia.co.uk explores new possibilities for navigation. The visitor is represented by an insect avatar, designed through a process of mutation, which then leads them left, right, down, up, over, and beyond …

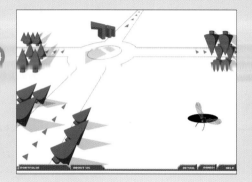

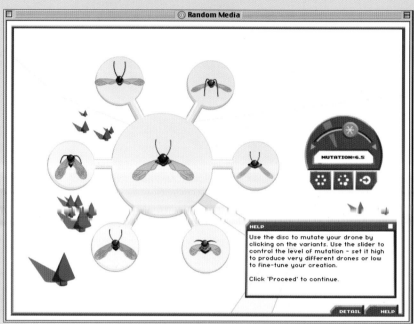

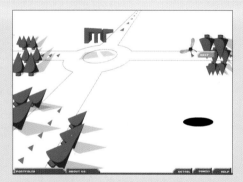

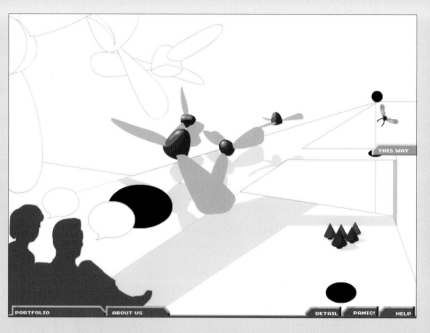

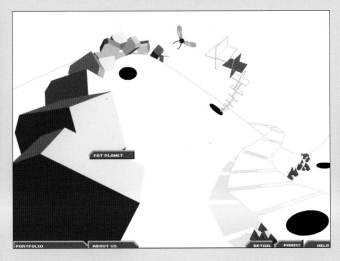
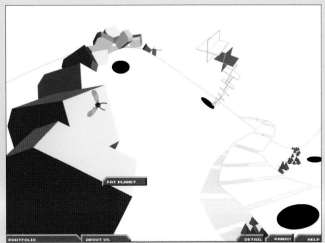

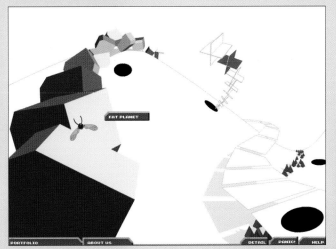
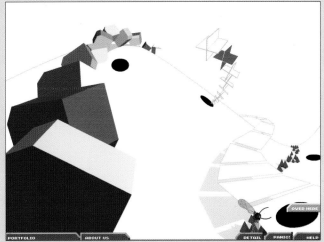

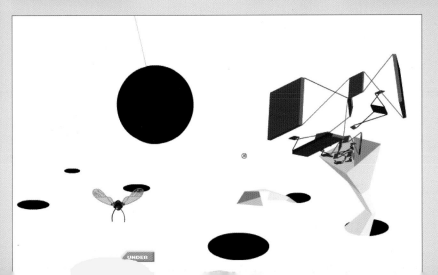

TURBULENCE: MORE-INC.

Www.turbulence.org is a net art exhibition site that commissions and supports net art. A recent addition to the site is the interactive Flash animated work More-Inc. by Wesley Meyer. As Turbulence explains on the site:

"More-Inc is an interactive simulator allowing users to explore questions of identity and happiness in a culture dominated by materialism and corporate control. The user's interactions and decisions lead to an experiential crescendo realized in breakdown, dissimulation, and resurrection."

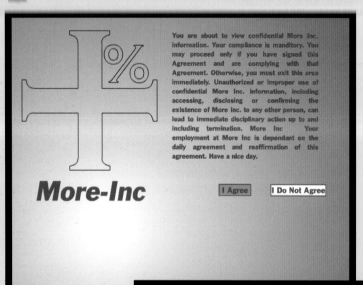

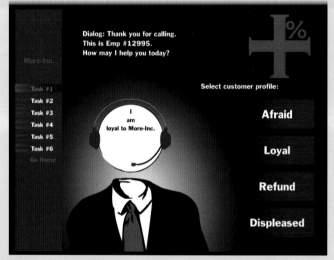

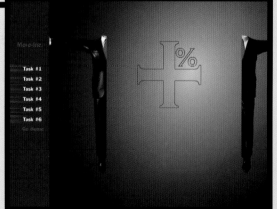

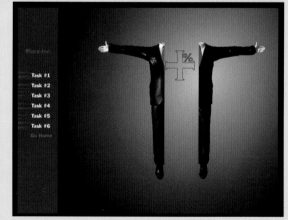

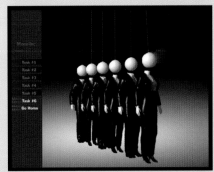

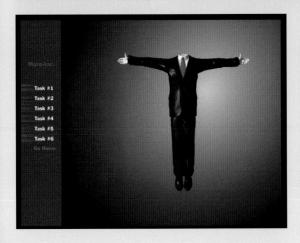

TURBULENCE: EMPTY VELOCITY

Angie Eng's work Empty Velocity, on display at www.turbulence.com/works, is interesting not only for its artistic ideas, but also as an exceptional demonstration of DHTML animation. Angie's introduction to the work starts:

"At high speed, the digital racer on his path runs into the sage preaching imaging power as the only limit to speed. For both, stationary position is the point of acceleration."

EMPTY VELOCITY

There are certain things that delight our body even while causing it a sort of pain, such as turning over in bed and changing sides well before that side is tired and constantly changing positions to cool off...Hence, men go on pointless trips and wander about faraway shores, fickle, never satisfied with the present, they try land one minute, the sea the next. They go on one trip after another from one spectacle to the next.

—Seneca

At high speed the digital racer on his path runs into the sage preaching imaging power as the only limit to speed. For both, stationary position is the point of acceleration.

You will learn to travel in time and space in stillness. You will appreciate the highest frequencies, from your body-internally to the City-externally; vibrations become finer and finer with an instantaneous transfer of energy. In emptiness you are open and closed simultaneously, ubiquitous in the world.

—Angie Eng, 1999

Site by Angie Eng. Sound by Angie Eng and Brian Moran.

Empty Velocity is a 1999 commission of New Radio and Performing Arts, Inc. of Staten Island for its Turbulence site. With funding from the Jerome Foundation.

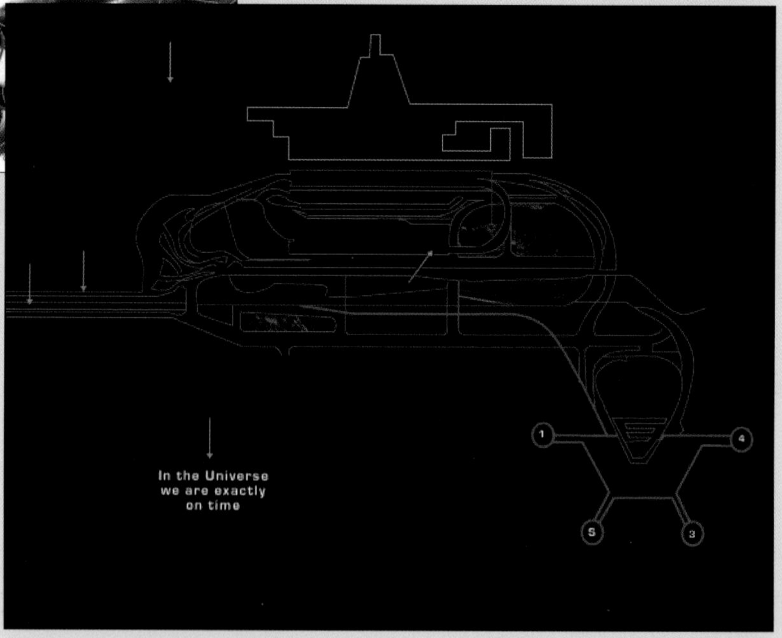

In the Universe
we are exactly
on time

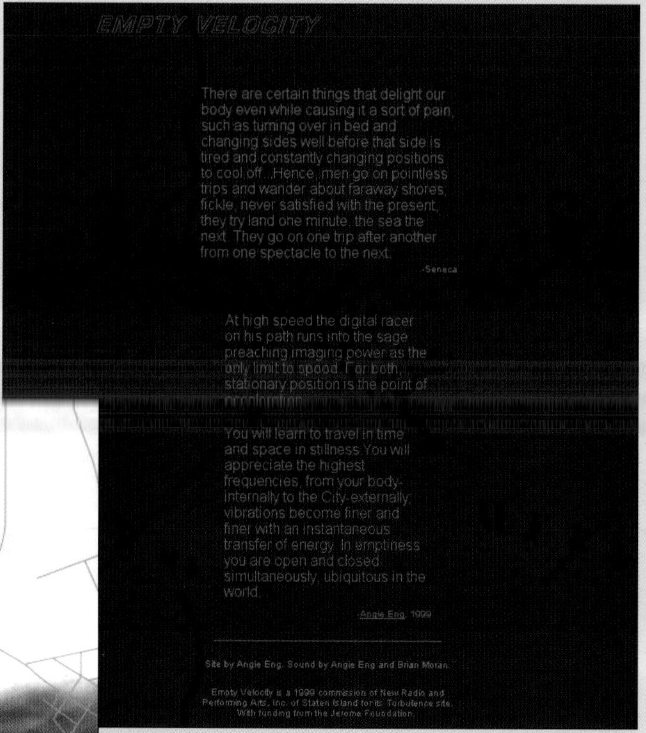

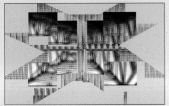

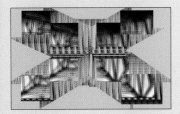

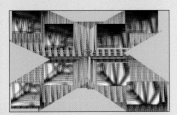

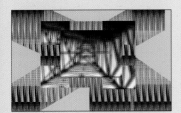

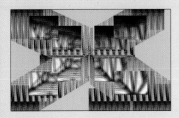

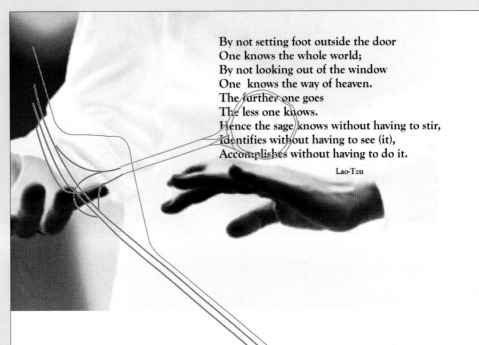

By not setting foot outside the door
One knows the whole world;
By not looking out of the window
One knows the way of heaven.
The further one goes
The less one knows.
Hence the sage knows without having to stir,
identifies without having to see (it),
Accomplishes without having to do it.

Lao-Tzu

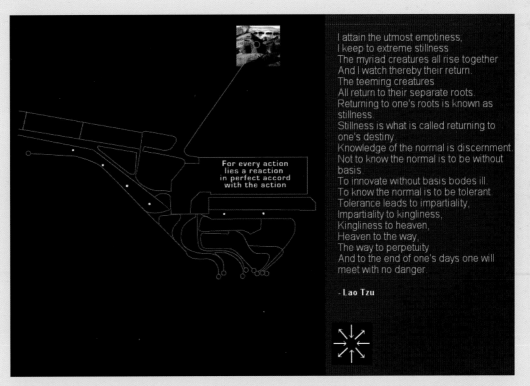

For every action
lies a reaction
in perfect accord
with the action

I attain the utmost emptiness;
I keep to extreme stillness
The myriad creatures all rise together
And I watch thereby their return.
The teeming creatures
All return to their separate roots.
Returning to one's roots is known as
stillness.
Stillness is what is called returning to
one's destiny.
Knowledge of the normal is discernment.
Not to know the normal is to be without
basis.
To innovate without basis bodes ill.
To know the normal is to be tolerant.
Tolerance leads to impartiality,
Impartiality to kingliness,
Kingliness to heaven,
Heaven to the way,
The way to perpetuity
And to the end of one's days one will
meet with no danger.

- Lao Tzu

BOWIENET

David Bowie's official Web site at www.davidbowie.com, which is designed by UltraStar and NettMedia, combines Flash navigational elements and animation with a delicate, understated coloring and design.

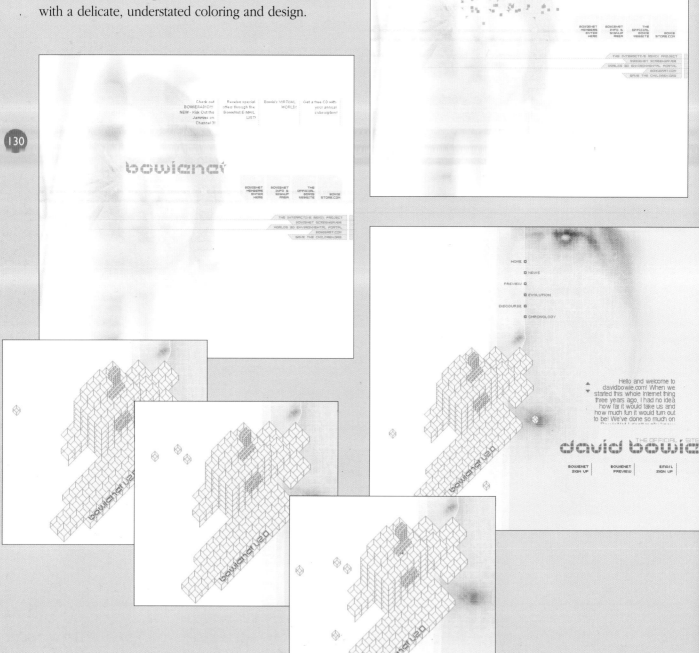

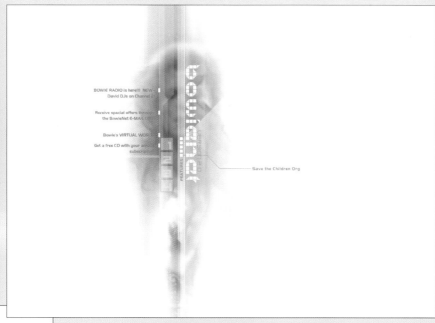

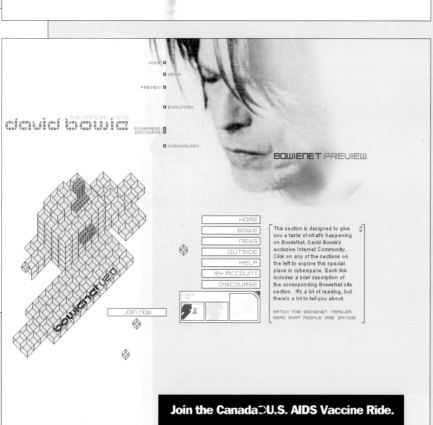

PRESSTUBE

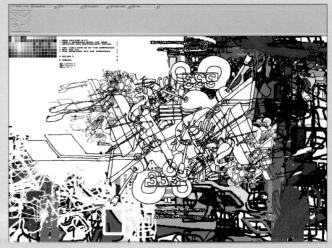

The Web site at www.presstube.com is an unusual and beautiful experimental Flash site by James Paterson, Eric Jensen, and Robbie Cameron, a joy for anyone interested in the possibilities of Web animation. Skilled drawing and advanced Flash scripting combine to produce some visually stunning and highly interactive animation. James Paterson says:

"Presstube is based on the idea of being the Web site that I would most like to go to. It is where all of my influences and experiences gel into something tangible."

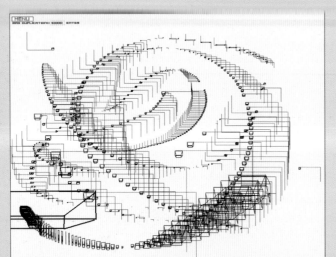

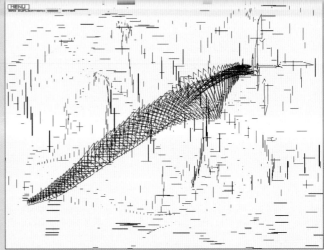

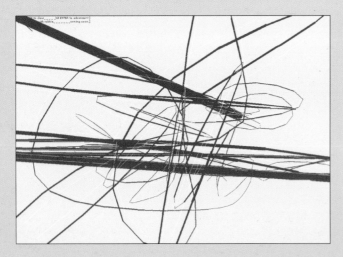

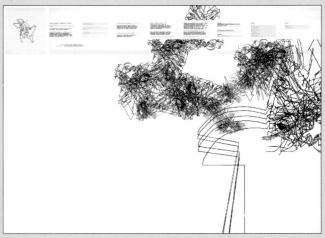

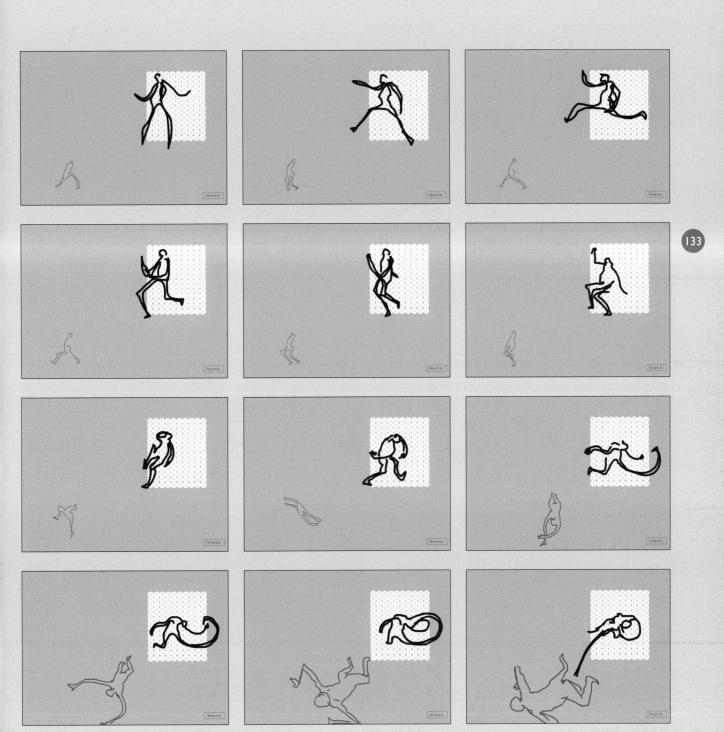

FLASH LOADING SEQUENCES

Flash loading sequences—the animated movies that entertain us at some sites while we are waiting for other material to download—can themselves be highly developed and sophisticated interactive works of Web animation. On the right is the simple but effective animation that reflects the character design in other parts of the site at www.ultrashock.com. Below is a typically bold and interactive loading sequence from www.presstube.com. On page 135 is the Flash sequence, which plays while the Shockwave game at mindstorms.lego.com is loading, which acts as a prelude for the game itself.

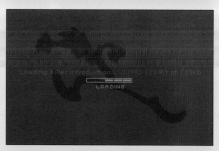

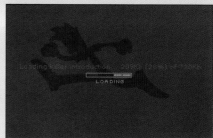

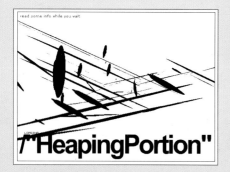

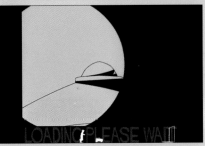

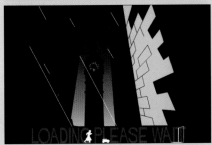

BABYLONHEADBOX

At www.babylonheadbox.fsnet.co.uk by Thomas Murphy, science is combined with Flash graphics and interactivity to produce a site that is interesting and unusual both in content and in form.

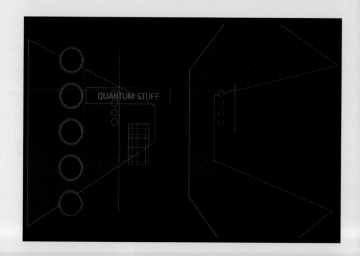

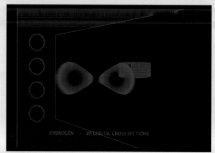

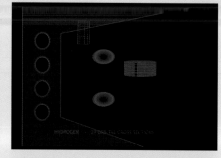

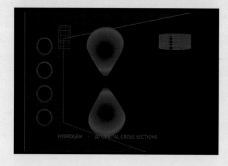

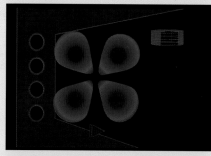

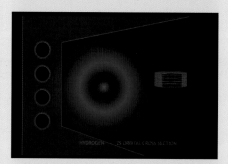

137

OBJECTS

WHAT'S GOING ON?

BOUNCY PLANETS

RES

x 336 y 195 x 105 y 10

This interactive star map should allow you to create most of the
views visible from the northern hemisphere.

The slider at the right controls the rotation of the sky and the two
buttons below control the magnification. Moving the mouse
over the edge of the star map will scroll it towards that edge.

HERCULES

EXIT

EXPLORATORIUM

San Francisco's Exploratorium, a world-famous science museum, offers a range of exciting and innovative interactive online experiences through its Web site at www.exploratorium.edu, which are mostly enabled by Shockwave. The visitor is encouraged to experiment and learn about optical illusions and other strange scientific phenomena through the use of inviting interactive elements embedded in the site.

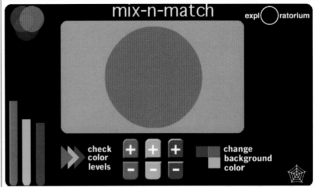

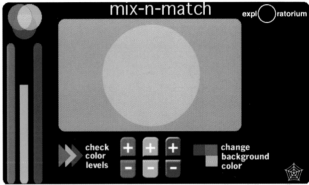

Mona

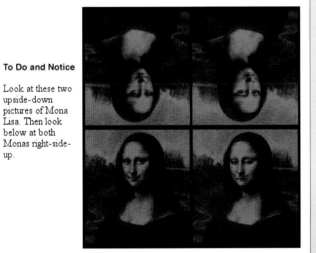

To Do and Notice

Look at these two upside-down pictures of Mona Lisa. Then look below at both Monas right-side-up.

SOUTH BANK CENTRE

London's South Bank Centre is a cultural venue of international standing. The Flash animation on its Web site at main.sbc.org.uk has to maintain a high level of aesthetic quality in combination with accurate and up-to-date information about events.

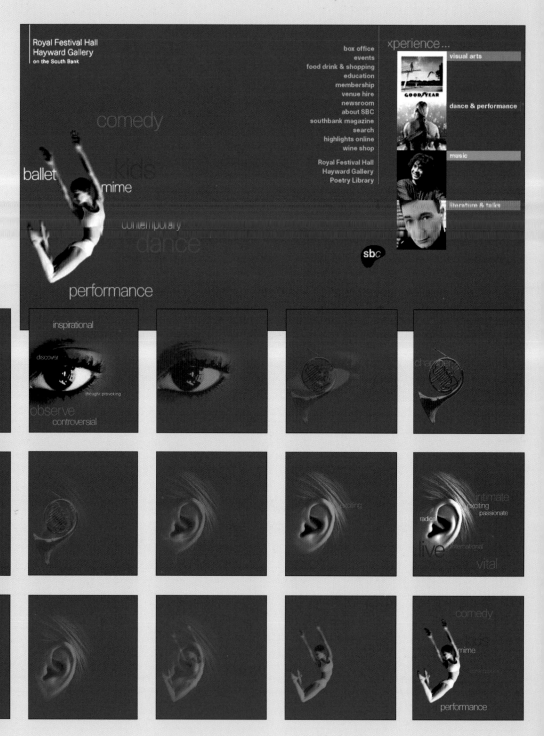

THE POWER STATION

Battersea Power Station has been a much talked-about feature of the London skyline for many years. Now a sophisticated interactive Shockwave web site designed by Random Media—www.thepowerstation.co.uk—brings its future potential to the notice of the whole world.

a visit for the day.
a weekend holiday.
or a permanent home.
experience what it means to be in the Power Station
be part of this new community of the Capital.

heart

loading...

enter main power station site

contact us | original shockwave trailer | planning application site

YOU HAVE REACHED THE OFFICIAL BATTERSEA POWER STATION WEB SITE.
YOU CAN EITHER VIEW THE MAIN POWER STATION SITE,
OR YOU CAN VIEW THE ORIGINAL SHOCKWAVE TRAILER
OR THE PLANNING APPLICATION WEB SITE
WHICH WAS LAUNCHED TO COINCIDE WITH THE GRANTING OF
DETAILED PLANNING PERMISSION ON THE 31 AUGUST 2000.

THIS SITE MAKES EXTENSIVE USE OF SHOCKWAVE TECHNOLOGY.
IF YOU DO NOT HAVE THE SHOCKWAVE PLUG-IN INSTALLED PLEASE CLICK HERE.

DESIGNED BY RANDOM MEDIA

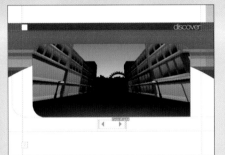  

 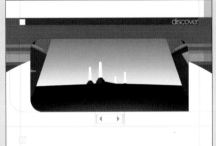 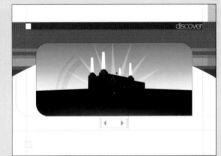

MOËT EXPLORER

Moët & Chandon's interactive Shockwave site www.moet.com/explorer, designed by Ici la Lune, uses travel around the world as a metaphor for navigation through hyperspace. The visitor—represented by a champagne cork—drifts from one country to another, visiting selected Web sites as they might visit tourist attractions.

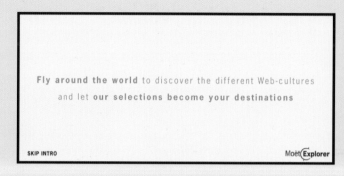

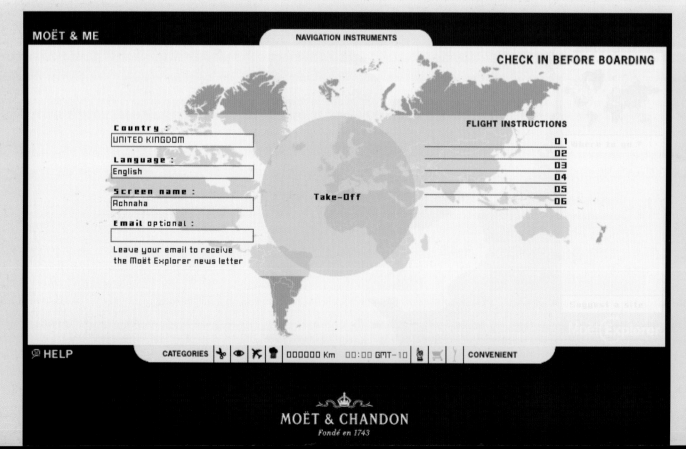

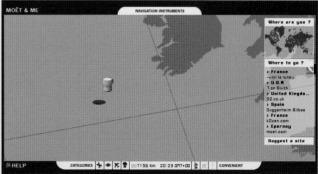

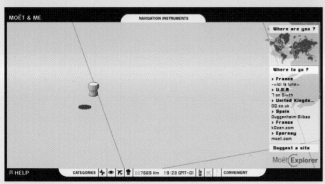

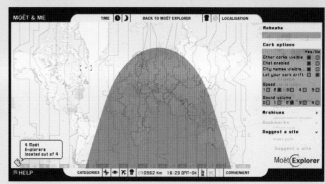

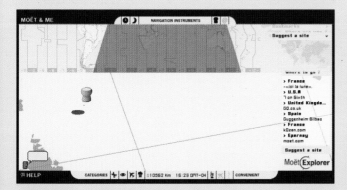

CRAYOLA®

Www.crayola.com is a suitably bright and cheerful site, animated by bold and colorful animated GIFs that are perfectly integrated into the pages by means of image slicing.

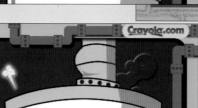

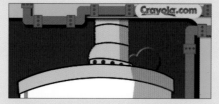

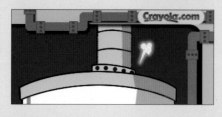

147

Crayola COLOR CENSUS 2000

The power of creativity.
Crayola®
It starts here.™

Home Products Send A Card Calendar Games   Search GO

PARENTS   EDUCATORS   CRAYOLA KIDS®

- Inspiring Ideas
- Card Creator
- The Crayola® Store.com
- Color Census
- Activity Book
- The Crayola FACTORY®
- Where To Buy?
- Helpful Information
- Media Center
- Crayola® Newsletter SUBSCRIBE NOW!

The final Crayola Color Census 2000 results are in! After counting and compiling more than 25,000 votes cast by crayon enthusiasts of all ages, results of the cyber-census reveal that kids and kids at heart alike are true blue when it comes to crayons. No re-count was necessary.

Color Census 2000 Winners! We've randomly selected 12 Crayola Color Census takers to receive one of the colorful prizes. Check out the winners' page.

Color Census Bureau -Official results of the virtual "Who's Hue" of Crayola crayon colors are in. Did purple mountain's majesty ascend higher than periwinkle? Is blue bell preferred over pine green? See for yourself, which colors topped the charts!

Celebrity Color Quiz - Is your favorite Crayola® color the same as Tiger Woods' or Mr. Roger's favorite?

Crayola Crayon Chronology - Check out the heritage of our hues. Everything you ever wanted to know about your favorite Crayola crayon color can be found here.

Color Quiz - Do you think you know a thing or two about true colors? Take this short quiz and see.

FUN WITH JAVA

Java is used for some very serious business on the Web, but it is also the perfect tool for animated fun. Its potential for creating constantly varying animations out of small elements make it suited to even the most economical Web sites.

Shown here to the right is www.qtzanimation.com, which offers fun animation free for the asking. Opposite, on the left, www.prominence.com/java/poetry offers do-it-yourself poetry composition from a selection of draggable words. To its right, on www.nofrontiere.com/nofrontierans the visitor can create a new creature by adapting one from the preexisting gallery.

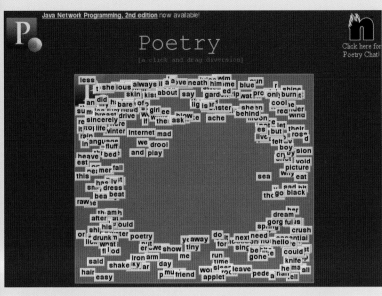

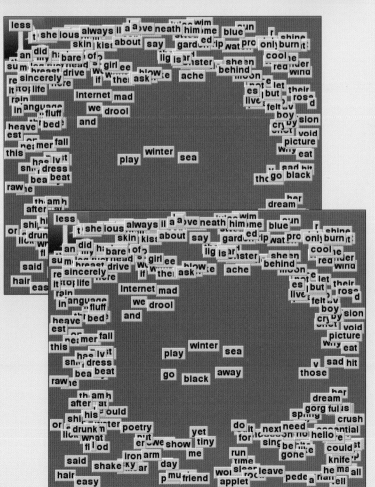

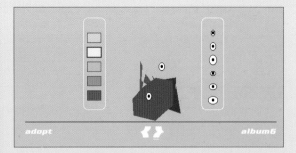

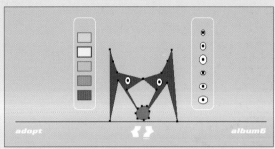

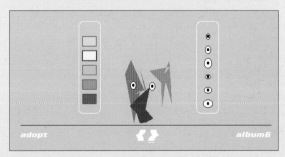

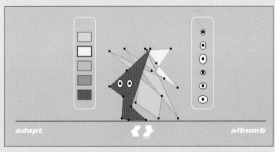

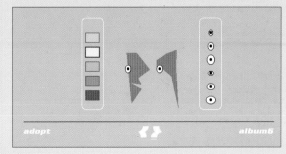

149

THE FORGE STUDIOS

The Forge Studios specializes in Poser animation, examples of which can be previewed as animated GIFs embedded in its Web site at www.the-forge.ie. The Forge's Web site and animations are created by a complex process in which Poser is used together with Bryce and Painter to create effective textures and environments for their animated figures.

150

WM TEAM

Www.wmteam.de is a fully animated Flash site with a distinctive character. The secret of its success lies in the integration of witty yet economical animation with effective presentation of key facts about the company—all achieved with humor and panache.

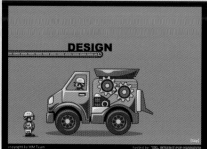
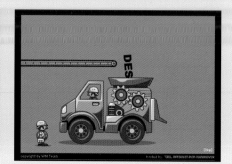

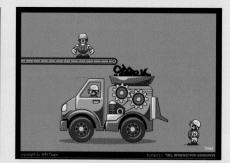

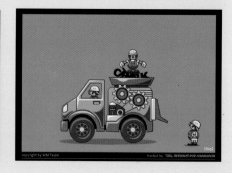

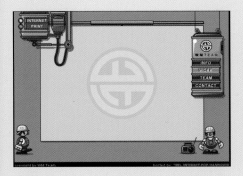
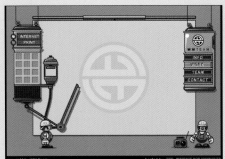
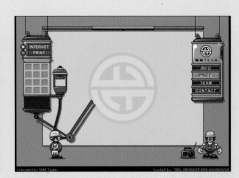
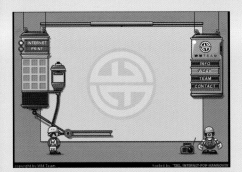
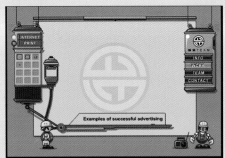
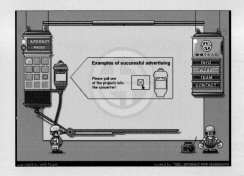
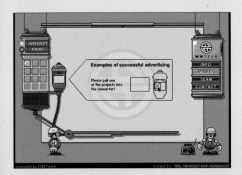

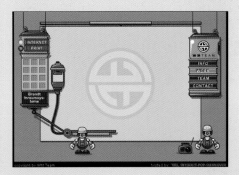
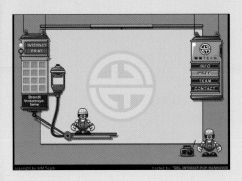

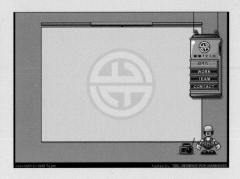

DLX DELUXE

DLX Deluxe is a skateboarding and snowboarding specialist retailer in Canada. Its Flash Web site, www.dlxdeluxe.com, designed by Blasfem Interactif, combines good functionality with quality and style and combines elegant animation with a design that reflects the nature of the company.

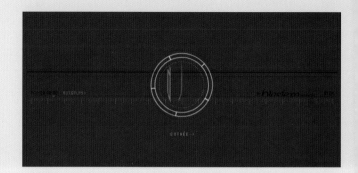

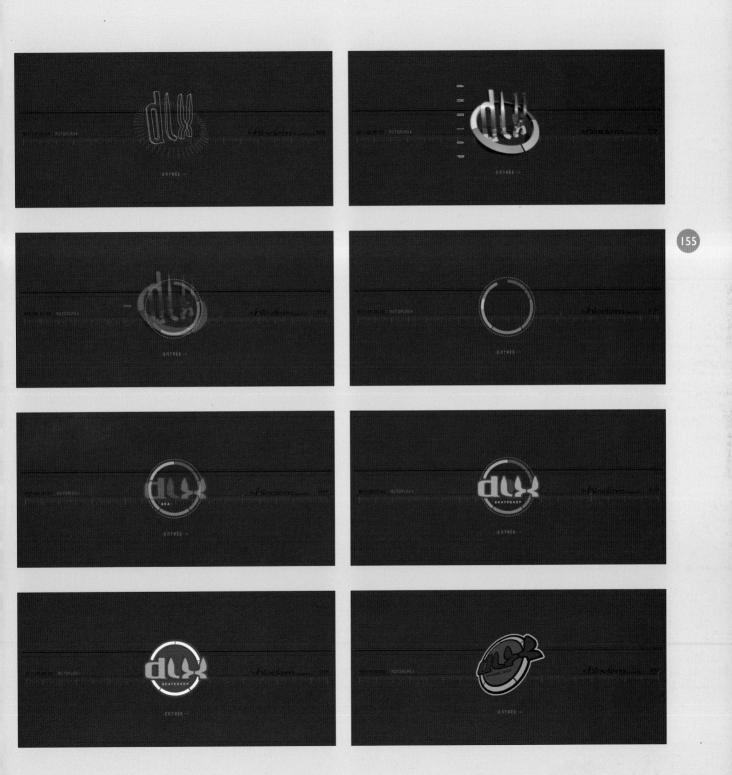

PRECINCT DESIGN LEGION

The Web site www.precinct.net is a well-known personal project by Swedish Web designer Daniel Achilles, proving that high-quality Web animation design may serve the needs of protest as well as commerce, entertainment, and art. The Save the World Issue and the Love Issue are illustrated here, both of which use Flash and some DHTML animation.

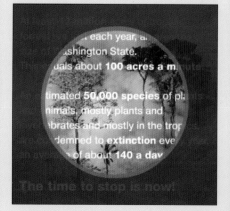

CREATIVE EDGE

The design company Creative Edge has created
an exciting fast-paced and stylish animated
introduction to its Flash Web site on their front door
page at www.8edge.com. Their striking use of a
limited monochrome palette with red detailing helps
to make the Flash movie visually effective even when
played at high speed.

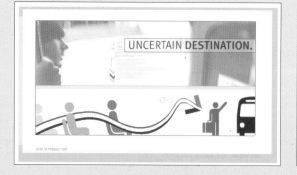

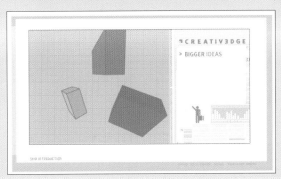

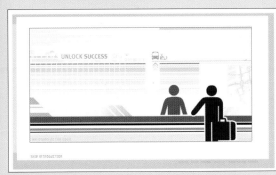

NISSAN DRIVEN

At Nissan's commercial Web site www.nissandriven.com the Future Driven pages feature Flash animation with unusual interface elements, which encourage the user to participate in the site experience. The loading sequences for the main pages are based on the appropriate metaphor of vehicles being assembled from a kit.

160

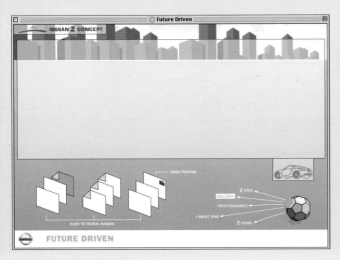

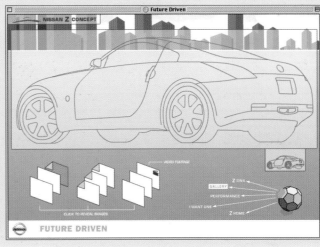

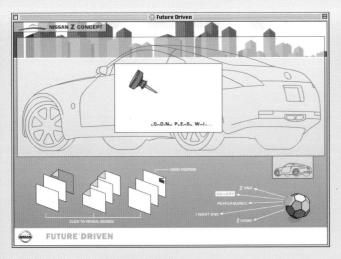

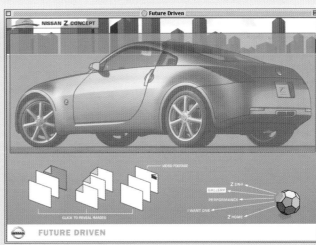

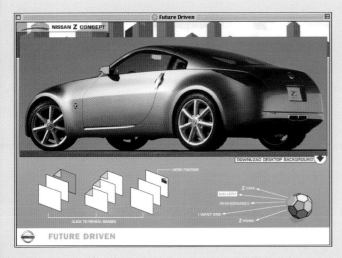

SWATCH

Www.swatch.com is a DHTML site that incorporates some Flash animated features. Remarkably, the clock puzzle keeps ticking even in its disassembled state!

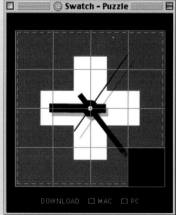

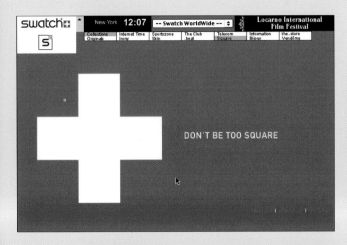
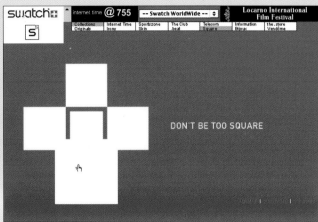

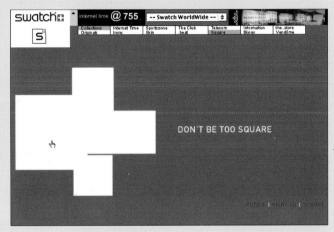
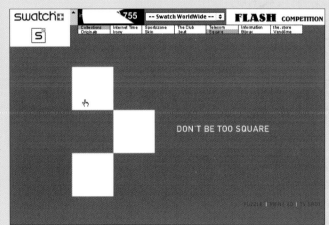
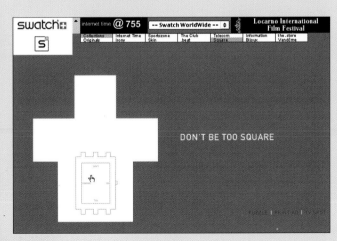
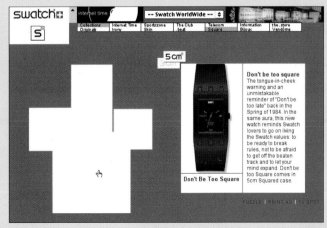

163

OMNIKONO

Www.omnikono.com is a German design site with strong color theming. Created in Flash, it features full-screen animation throughout, with interesting touches of interactivity, such as background color changes controlled through the handset on the SCI pages.

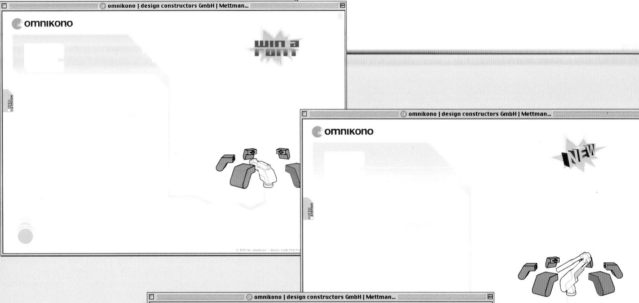

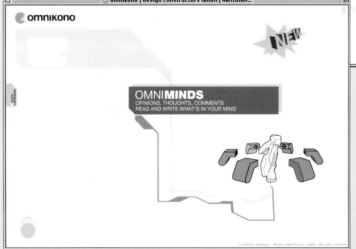

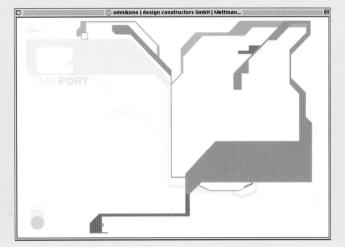

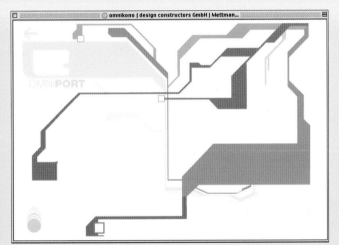

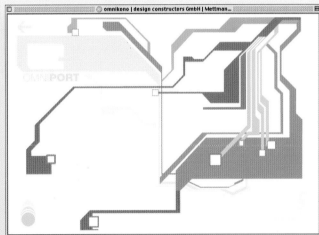

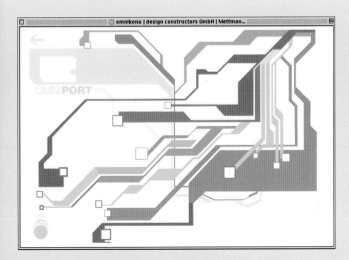

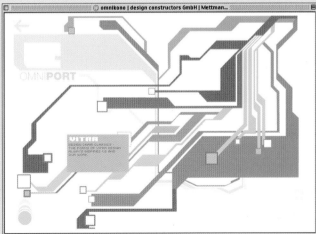

CHANEL

Chanel's Web site www.chanel.com uses Flash to create very smooth transitions throughout the featured animations in an elegantly classic style, which is appropriate to the image of this world-famous French couture house. The site is designed to inform as well as to sell, to which ends it contains interesting archive photos and historical details, all smoothly presented by means of Flash.

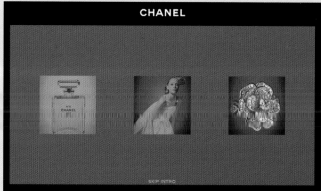

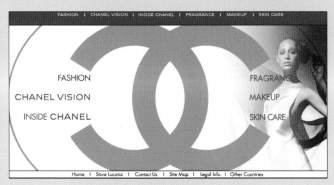
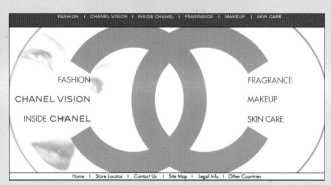

ULTRASHOCK

The Web site www.ultrashock.
com is an Internet resource and
meeting-point site for multimedia
designers and the Flash community.
Made especially to impress visitors,
its series of large-scale introductory
Flash movies feature bright cartoon
graphics imposed on the Ultrashock
livery gray background.

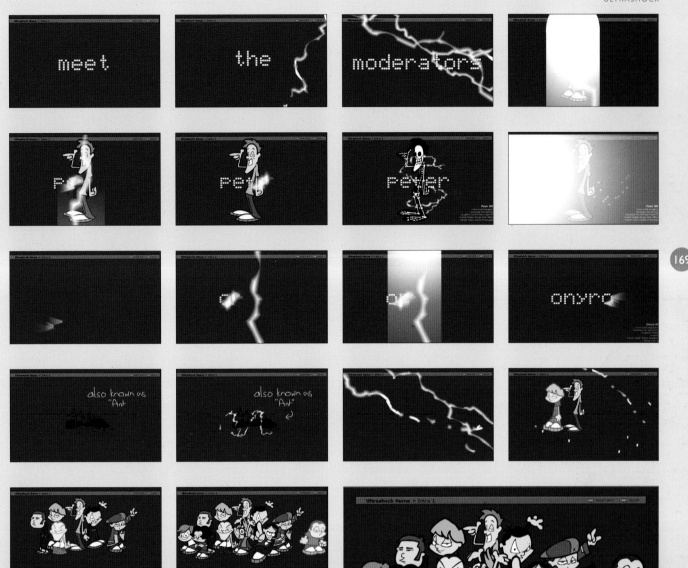

AARDMAN ANIMATIONS

Aardman Animations Ltd. grew from humble beginnings in the 1970s to become one of the world's leading model animation studios and multiple Oscar winners. But their Web site at www.aardman.com remains charming, welcoming, and packed with information about all things Aardman. It features a series of outstanding animated GIFs of Morph and friends.

Aardman History ✳ Meet The People ✳ Check Our Job Opportunities ✳ FAQ's

Model Making

* Front Of House
* Production
* Canteen
* Creatives
* Lighting & Cameras
* Model Making
* Studio
* Feature Film Set
* Edit

Model Making

Click to see the large picture...

✳ Wallace & Gromit ✳
✳ Rex The Runt ✳
✳ Chicken Run ✳
✳ Angry Kid ✳

QTVR

400K

Model making is one of our most popular areas for visitors; it's where our characters come to life.

Our process starts as a director comes through from creatives department with 2d designs and from this our model makers sculpt and mould a 3d 'maquette' or prototype, usually in plasticene. This is then modified, adapted and fine-tuned. We can use this maquette to make a mould and cast pieces in different materials to create the puppet that can be animated.

We use a variety of materials in our workshop, plasticine, silicone/rubber, resin, foam latex, sculpey, milliput, and the list goes on, according to the requirements for particular characters. We use armatures made of ball and socket pieces (plates and drilled stainless steel balls) soldered/brazed to rods to create a metal skeleton. We use armatures in all our characters now, except very small incidental puppets, however, Morph has never had an armature, he is solid plasticine.

Our characters generally have plasticine heads allowing easy manipulation and animation of expression, other materials are used for the rest of the puppet. With animated speech, if there is only a small amount of expression from the character an animator may sculpt the mouth shapes on the puppet's head, however, if more speech is required we will make mouth replacements. A separate mouth is sculpted for each consonant and vowel and the animator replaces each mouth, to achieve different word shapes and blends the plasticine to hide the seams.

We don't build sets or props in house, with the exception of immediate props like hats or suitcases and occasionally animatable props. The sets and props are built usually by specialist local companies.

From here it's into the studio for the shoot.

Showcase
Films, TV, Music Vids

* Stage Fright
* Pop
* Wat's Pig
* The Morph Files
* A Close Shave
* Pib and Pog
* The Wrong Trousers
* Loves Me... Loves Me Not
* Adam
* A Grand Day Out
* Spice Girls – Viva Forever

Back Next

Aztec Shorts – Chunga Chui (Leopard Beware)

Title: Chunga Chui – Leopard Beware
Year: 2000
Running Time: 1 minute 35 seconds
Gauge: 35mm
Sound: Stereo

More Showcase information...
Credits

Chunga Chui

An African herdsman performs a tribal dance to ward off the evil spirit of the predatory Leopard.

Written, Animated and Directed by Stefano Cassini.

* Wallace & Gromit *
* Rex The Runt *
* Chicken Run *
* Angry Kid *

AARDMARKET.COM
cracking animation
Order Online

© Aardman Animations Ltd. 2000

Showcase
Films, TV, Music Vids

Lip Synch Series:
* Next
* Ident
* Going Equipped
* Creature Comforts
* War Story
* Nina Simone – My Baby Just Cares For Me
* Babylon
* Peter Gabriel – Sledgehammer

Back Next

Lip Synch Series – Creature Comforts

Send this as a postcard

Polar Bears

Year: 1989
Running Time: 5 minutes
Gauge: 35mm
Ratio: 1:133

A series of interviews with the animals in an English Zoo. Used to open spaces and sunnier climates, they comment on accommodation, diet and, of course, the English weather.

More Showcase information...
Credits & Awards

Watch it online

Click to see the large picture...

* Wallace & Gromit *
* Rex The Runt *
* Chicken Run *
* Angry Kid *

AARDMARKET.COM
Buy this Film on DVD & VHS
Order Online

© Channel Four/Aardman Animations Ltd 1989

171

TYPOGRAPHIC

TypogRaphic advertise unashamedly gratuitous animation at their Flash Web site www.typographic.com. Their experimental approach continues to help all Web animation artists and designers to explore the potential for Flash animation in general, and the animation of text in particular.

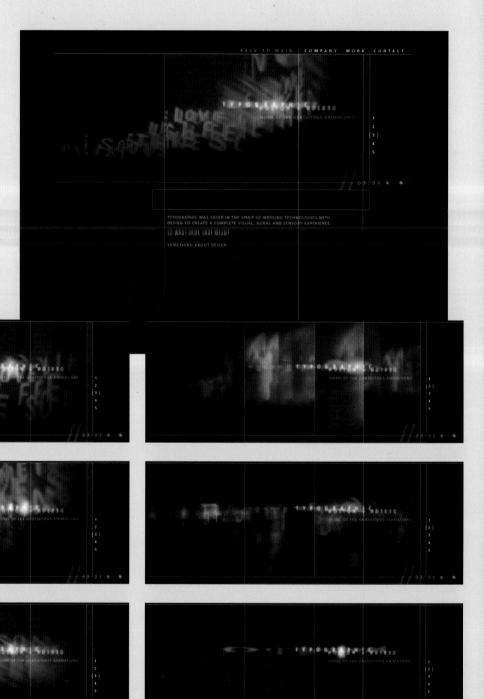

OPEN STUDIO

Open Studio is an exciting interactive animation and online drawing facility created in Java by artist Andy Deck. By connecting to draw.artcontext.net, up to nine users at a time can create collaborative works online with unusual drawing tools or play back an animated record of recent activity. The illustrations shown here are drawn from a live experimental interaction between Andy and myself.

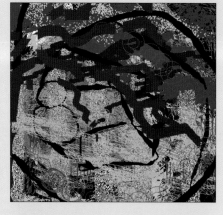

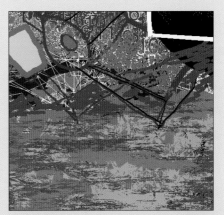

176

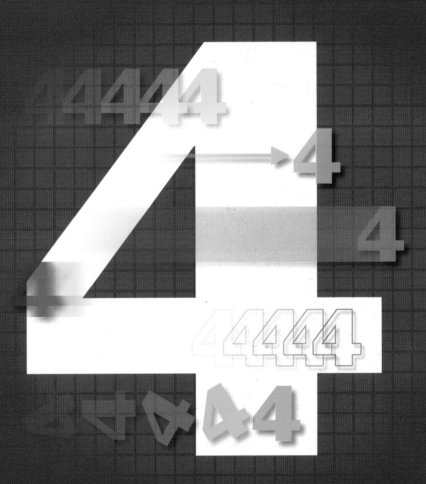

USEFUL SOURCES

BOOKS

The Animation Book (New Digital Edition)
Kit Laybourne
Three Rivers Press, 1998

Although still aimed at animated film-making, this nevertheless remains the book on how to make animation.

Digital Media Tools
Nigel Chapman and Jenny Chapman
John Wiley & Sons Ltd, 2001

A thorough practical introduction to Photoshop, ImageReady, Flash, Illustrator, Dreamweaver, and Premiere, with practice exercises throughout and CD-ROM demos.

Dust or Magic: Secrets of Successful Multimedia Design.
Bob Hughes
Addison-Wesley, 1999

Lots to think about for anyone interested in interactive multimedia design. A book to read rather than look at.

Effective Web Animation
J. Scott Hamlin
Addison-Wesley, 1999

Not up to date with the latest technologies, but still a good source, with plenty of useful advice and information.

Experimental Animation: Origins of a New Art
Robert Russett and Cecile Starr
Da Capo Press Inc., 1976

A classic and inspirational survey of the work of great experimental animators of the past. Just as relevant to experimental Web animation as to traditional forms.

New Masters of Flash
Various authors
Friends of Ed, 2000

A large and fascinating book containing case studies and personal essays by advanced Flash designers. The work-throughs are not for beginners: they contain serious ActionScript and advanced techniques.

PREVIOUS DESIGN DIRECTORIES

Digital 3D Design
Simon Danaher
Watson-Guptill, New York, 2001

This book explains the use of 3D applications in digital graphic design.

Icon Design
Steve Caplin
Watson-Guptill, New York, 2001

This beautifully illustrated book explains the use of graphic icons in computer interface design.

www.color
Roger Pring
Watson-Guptill, New York, 2000

Provides guidance on effective use of color in designing Web sites.

Digital Diagrams
Trevor Bounford
Watson-Guptill, New York, 2000

Shows how to produce effective design and presentation of statistical information.

www.layout
Gerry Glenwright
Watson-Guptill, New York, 2001

A highly illustrated book that shows how to create effective design and layout for the World Wide Web.

RESOURCE WEB SITES

javaboutique.internet.com
Large, serious Java resource site, with lots to download including animation applets and games.

memory.loc.gov/ammem/oahtml/oahome.html
Delve into the earliest days of animation with this remarkable online collection—the Origins of American Animation (from 1900 to 1921), at the U.S. Library of Congress site. You can even download these rare early animations to disk.

useit.com
See what the influential designer Jakob Nielsen has to say about usability and interface design (and Flash), and then arrive at your own conclusions.

webreference.com/3d/
Lots of online lessons in 3D Web animation, plus links, etc.

www.adobe.com/web/gallery/main.html
Interviews and articles on Web designers, with links to their work.

www.agag.com
Official site of the Animated Gifs Artists' Guild, with a wide range of resources, a gallery, and links.

www.dhtmlcentral.com
An expanding DHTML resource site with free scripts.

www.flashkit.com/welcome.shtml
The world's largest Flash resource site; includes Open Source movies.

www.linkdup.com
An excellent starting point for exploring the world of Web animation.

www.macromedia.com/software
The starting point for a wide range of links connected with all of Macromedia's software and the Web sites made with it.

www.redsheep.com
The GIF side of the site has a useful tutorial on making animated GIFs by a member of the Animated Gif Artists' Guild, together with plenty of examples and links.

www.surfstation.lu
Inspiration for designers, with plenty of links.

www.ultrashock.com
A focus point for multimedia developers and the Flash community.

www.web3d.org/vrml/vrml.htm/
Covers 3D in general as well as VRML, despite the name.

PROMOTIONAL SITES

www.absolut.com
www.cartier.com
www.ecko.com/plex/
www.evian.com
www.frosties.co.uk
www.guinness.com
www.rolex.com
www.switchbev.com
www.wonka.co.uk

DESIGN AND MEDIA HOUSE SITES

www.dform1shiftfunc.net
www.digitalorganism.com
www.freestyleinteractive.com
www.practicedesign.co.uk
www.wireframe.co.za

CULTURAL AND EDUCATIONAL SITES

www.motown.com/classicmotown/
www.nationalgeographic.com/congotrek360/
www.nhm.ac.uk/museum
www.sfmoma.org
www.si.edu/revealingthings/
www.willing-to-try.com

ART, DESIGN, AND EXPERIMENTAL SITES

http://surface.yugop.com
www.kozen.com/EN/alchimie/alchimie.htm
www.mindsway.com
www.modifyme.com
www.theremediproject.com
www.vispo.com/animisms

ANIMATION, CARTOON, AND GAMES SITES

www2.warnerbros.com/web
www.atomfilms.com
www.deathbyjargon.com
www.homestarrunner.com
www.randomhouse.com/seussville/
www.shockwave.com
www.vectorpark.com

GLOSSARY

3D Three dimensional, that is, an effect to give the illusion of depth on a flat page or monitor screen.

algorithm A predetermined procedure for solving a specific problem.

aliasing The term describing the jagged appearance of bitmapped images or fonts either when the resolution is insufficient or when they have been enlarged. This is caused by the pixels—which are square with straight sides—making up the image becoming visible.

animated GIF A GIF file containing more than one image. Many programs, including Web browsers, will display each of the images in turn, thus producing an animation. The delay between frames and the number of times the animation should loop can be specified in the file. The animated GIF is the only file format for animated sequences that does not depend upon the presence of a browser plug-in for playback on Web pages.

animatic A sequence of key still images from an animation, which are organized and played back in a time-based medium, such as video, to give an idea of the pacing of the animation and the development of narrative, etc. Sound may be added to an animatic to help assess pacing and synchronization. An animatic is often a filmed version of a storyboard, in which each key image is held for the length of time that the sequence it represents is planned to take.

animation The term is derived from "animate," meaning to give life to, or bring alive. Traditionally, animation has meant the creation of the illusion of movement by means of taking still photographs of something that is changed between shots on to film-stock or video-tape, one frame at a time. A very wide range of techniques has been devised to create that illusion of movement between frames that becomes animation when the film is played back.

animation techniques have ranged from the photography of actual moving objects or people, a single frame at a time (pixelation), through the manipulation of plasticine or other 3D figures, to the familiar and widely used drawing of cartoon figures—with many other techniques in between. Since the advent of digital technology, the definition of animation has become broader. In the context of the World Wide Web animation may now be taken to mean any technique that brings Web pages to life through movement or change, by means of images that are created or computed frame by frame.

antialias/antialiasing A technique of optically eliminating the jagged effect of bitmapped images or text reproduced on low-resolution devices such as monitors. This is achieved by adding pixels of an in-between tone—the edges of the object's color are blended with its background by averaging the density of the range of pixels involved. Antialiasing is also sometimes employed to filter texture maps, such as those used in 3D applications, to prevent moiré patterns.

applet Although a general term that can be applied to a small application that performs a specific task, such as the calculator, an applet is normally used to describe a application written in the Java programming language, which is downloaded by an Internet browser to perform specific tasks.

artwork In animation, drawings, paintings, photographs, and any other graphic materials, in either physical or digital media, that are prepared for use in a work of animation.

background The area of an image on which the principal subject or foreground sits. It may be colored to give extra definition to the image.

bandwidth The measure of the speed at which information is passed between two points, which may be between modems, or across a "bus," or from memory to disk—the broader the bandwidth, the faster data flows.

banner An image on a web page, usually at the top, which deliberately attracts attention, generally for advertising purposes.

Bézier curve A curve whose shape is defined by a pair of "direction lines" at each end, which specify the direction and rate at which the curve leaves or enters the corresponding end point. Drawing programs usually allow you to draw Bézier curves by dragging out the direction lines with a pen tool, and to adjust them by pulling their ends. Bézier curves can be joined together smoothly by lining up direction lines where the curves meet, so they can be used to make complicated smoothly curving paths. they are also used to specify the values of interpolated properties in tweened animation. They can be extended into three dimensions and are used as motion paths for objects, cameras, and lights in 3D animation programs.

bit A contraction of binary digit, the smallest piece of information a computer can use. A bit is expressed as one of two values, which can be a 1 or 0.

bit depth The number of bits assigned to each pixel on a monitor, scanner, or image file. One-bit, for example, will only produce black and white (the bit is either on or off), while 8-bit will generate 256 grays or colors (256 is the maximum number of permutations of a string of eight 1s and 0s), and 24-bit will produced 16.7 million colors (256 × 256 × 256).

bitmap An array of values specifying the color of every pixel in a digital image.

bitmapped graphic An image made up of dots, or pixels, and usually generated by "paint" or "image-editing" applications, as distinct from the "vector" images of "object-oriented" drawing applications.

browser An application enabling you to view, or "browse," World Wide Web pages across the Internet.

button see **navigation button**

byte A single group made up of eight bits (0s and 1s), which is processed as one unit. It is possible to configure eight 0s and 1s in only 256 different permutations, thus a byte can represent any value between 0 and 255.

cache (pron.: cash) A small area of memory (RAM) set aside for the temporary storage of frequently accessed data.

CAD abb. computer-aided design. Strictly speaking, any design carried out using a computer, but the term is generally used with reference to 3D design, where a computer software application is used to construct and develop complex structures.

caption This used to mean a headline printed above an illustration identifying its contents. Nowadays, however, a caption is generally used to mean any descriptive text that accompanies illustrative matter, and should, more accurately, be described as a "legend."

Cartesian coordinate system A geometry system employed in any number of dimensions, from 2D upward. It uses numbers to locate a point on a plane in relation to an origin where one or more points intersect.

cascading style sheet see **CSS**

cel In nondigital animation, a sheet of transparent acetate on which images for animation are drawn and painted. Cels may be overlaid on one another and on a background scene to allow the independent animation of different characters. The traditional technique of cel animation is closely echoed in many digital animation applications where animation is created on many different layers and transparency used to overlay the images.

client (1) see **client-server**

client (2) A term loosely used to refer to a computer running a client program.

client-server The model of interaction in a distributed system, such as the Internet, in which a program running on one computer sends a request to a program running on another computer and waits for a response. The program sending the request is called a client. The program sending the response is called the server.

clipping Limiting an image to within the bounds of a particular area.

clipping path A Bézier outline that defines which area of an image should be considered transparent or "clipped." This lets you isolate the foreground object and is particularly useful when images are to be placed over new backgrounds.

clipping plane In 3D applications, a plane beyond which an object is not visible. A view of the world has six clipping planes: top, bottom, left, right, hither, and yon.

CLUT abb. color look-up table. A preset table of colors (to a maximum of 256 colors) that the operating system uses when in 8-bit mode. CLUTS are also attached to individual images saved in 8-bit "indexed" mode—that is, when an application converts a 24-bit image (one with millions of colors) to 8-bit, it draws up a table ("index") of up to 256 colors (the total number of colors depends on where the image will be viewed, Mac, Windows, or Web, for example) of those most frequently used in the image. So if a color in the original image does not appear in the table, the application chooses the closest one or simulates it by "dithering" available colors in the table.

color depth This is the number of bits required to define the color of each pixel. For example, only one bit is required to display a black and white image, while an 8-bit image can display either 256 grays or 256 colors, and a 24-bit image displays 16.7 million colors – eight bits each for red, green, and blue (256 × 256 × 256).

compression The technique of rearranging data so that it either occupies less space on disk or transfers faster between devices or on communication lines. Different kinds of compression techniques are employed for different kinds of data.

181

Applications, for example, must not lose any data when compressed, while photographic images and movies can tolerate a certain amount of data loss. Compression methods that do not lose data are referred to as "lossless," while "lossy" is used to describe methods in which some data is lost. Movies and animations employ techniques called "codecs" (compression/ decompression). There are many proprietary utilities for compressing data.

cross-platform The term applied to software, multimedia titles, or anything else (such as floppy disks) that will work on more than one computer platform, that is, those that run different operating systems, such as the Macintosh OS or Microsoft Windows.

CSS *abb.* Cascading Style Sheets. A language defined by a World Wide Web Consortium recommendation for specifying the appearance (fonts, positioning, color, etc.) of the elements of an HTML document.

cursor The name for the blinking marker that indicates the current working position in a document. For example, the point in a line of text at which the next character will appear when you strike a key on the keyboard. The cursor may be represented by a small vertical line or block and is not to be confused with the "pointer"—the marker that indicates the current position of the mouse.

data Although strictly speaking the plural of "datum," meaning a piece of information, "data" is now used as a singular noun to describe—particularly in the context of computers—more or less anything that can be stored or processed, whether it be a single bit, a chunk of text, an image, a piece of audio and so on.

data graphic Any visual representation of data.

data transfer rate The speed of data transmitted across communications networks, measured in bits per second (bps).

DHTML see **Dynamic HTML**

dial-up The term describing a connection to the Internet or to a network, which is made by dialing a telephone number for access.

digital Anything operated by or created from information or signals represented by digits, such as in digital recording, as distinct from analogue, in which information is represented by a physical variable. (In a recording this may be via the grooves in a vinyl platter.)

digitize, digitalize To convert anything, such as text, images, or sound, into binary form.

dither(ed), dithering A term used to refer to the use of patterns of pixels of available colors, for example, the colors in a Web "safe" palette, to simulate missing colors, based upon the principle of optical mixing. Dithered images often have a "dotty" appearance when closely inspected; reminiscent of post-Impressionist paintings by Seurat and other artists who also employed the principle of optical mixing.

download To transfer data from a remote computer, such as an Internet server, to your own. The opposite of upload.

draw(ing) application Drawing applications can be defined as those that are object-oriented (they use "vectors" to mathematically define lines and shapes), as distinct from painting applications, which use pixels to make images ("bitmapped graphics"). Some applications combine both.

drop shadow A shadow projected onto the background behind an image or character, designed to lift the image or character off the surface.

Dynamic HTML A term loosely used to refer to the combination of JavaScript, CSS, and basic HTML code, which enables you to add features including animation and rollover buttons to Web pages without relying on browser plug-ins or Java coding.

e-commerce Commercial transactions conducted electronically over a network or the Internet.

file format The way a program arranges data so that it can be stored or displayed on a computer. This can range from the file format used uniquely by a particular application, to those that are used by many different software programs. In order to help you work on a job that requires the use of several applications, or to work with other people who may be using different applications from yours, file formats tend to be standardized. Common file formats are TIFF and JPEG for bitmapped image files, EPS for object-oriented image files and ASCII for text files.

Flash (Macromedia) Software for creating vector graphics and animations for Web presentations. Flash generates small files, which are correspondingly quick to download and, being vector, are scalable to any dimension without an increase in the file size.

fps *abb.* frames per second. The units in which frame-rate is most often specified.

frame (1) In animation, a single image that is part of an animated sequence. Originally a frame was one of a series of individual exposures on a strip of movie film, but the term is now used more broadly to indicate a single still image that is part of an animated sequence in any medium.

frame (2) On the Web, a means of displaying more than one page at a time within a single window. The window is divided into separate areas ("frames"), each one displaying a separate page. A common use of frames is to display a menu that remains static while other parts of the web page—displayed in the same window—contain information that can, for example, be "scrolled."

frame-rate The speed at which the individual frames of an animation are substituted for one another, that is, the speed at which the animation is played. This rate is usually specified as a number of frames per second, but may be indicated in another way, for example, by delay between the substitution of frames, expressed in hundredths of a second, in animated GIFs.

free form shape A shape that is not regular or geometric.

GIF *abb.* graphics interchange format. One of the main bitmapped image formats used on the Internet. Devised by CompuServe, an Internet Service Provider (now part of AOL), thus sometimes (although rarely) referred to as "CompuServe GIF," GIF is a 256-color format with two specifications, GIF87a and, more

recently, GIF89a, the latter providing additional features such as transparent backgrounds. The GIF format uses a "lossless" compression technique, or "algorithm," and thus does not squeeze files as much as the JPEG format, which is "lossy" (some data is discarded). For use in Web browsers JPEG is the format of choice for tone images, such as photographs, while GIF is more suitable for line images and other graphics, such as text.

Gourand shading A method of rendering by manipulating colors and shades selectively along the lines of certain vertices, which are then averaged across each polygon face in order to create a realistic light and shade effect.

Graphics Interchange Format see **GIF**

grayscale The rendering of an image, either fore- or background, in a range of grays from white to black. In a digital image and on a computer monitor this usually means that an image is rendered with eight bits assigned to each pixel, giving a maximum of 256 levels of gray. Monochrome monitors (used increasingly rarely nowadays) can only display black pixels, in which case, grays are achieved by varying the number and positioning of black pixels using the technique called dithering.

HTML *abb.* Hypertext Markup Language. A text-based "page description language" (PDL) used to format documents published on the World Wide Web, which can be viewed with web browsers.

image slicing The practice of dividing up a digital image into rectangular areas or slices, which can then be optimized or animated independently for efficient

Web presentation. Programs that enable you to slice images automatically generate an HTML code that puts the slices back together on a Web page.

in-between see **tween(ing)**

indexed color An image mode of a maximum of 256 colors that is used in some applications, such as Adobe Photoshop, to reduce the file size of RGB images, so that they can be used, for example, in multimedia presentations or Web pages. This is achieved by using an indexed table of colors ("a color look-up table," or CLUT) to which the colors in an image are matched. If a color in the image does not appear in the table (which can be either an existing table using a known palette of "safe" colors or one constructed from an image), then the application selects the nearest color or simulates it by arranging the available colors in a pattern (known as dithering).

interactive animation Animation that varies, develops, or responds as a direct result of some user input, such as a mouse or keyboard event.

interface see **user interface**

interpolation A computer calculation used to estimate unknown values that fall between known ones. One use of this process is to redefine pixels in bitmapped images after they have been modified in some way, for instance, when an image is resized (called "resampling") or rotated, or if color corrections have been made. In such cases the program takes estimates from the known values of other pixels lying in the same or similar ranges. Interpolation is also used by some scanning and image-manipulation

183

software to enhance the resolution of images that have been scanned at low resolution. Some applications allow you to choose an interpolation method. Photoshop, for example, offers Nearest Neighbor (for fast but imprecise results, which may produce jagged effects), Bilinear (for medium-quality results), and Bicubic (for smooth and precise results, but with slower performance). The insertion of animation values between two keyframes of a movie sequence (for example, tweening) is also interpolation.

inverse kinematics A method of animating structures that form a chain of links, such as a human arm. The position of all the elements in the chain, for example, forearm, elbow, upper arm, etc., are computed to fit the position of the final element—in this example, the hand.

ISDN *abb.* Integrated Services Digital Network. A telecommunication technology that transmits data on special digital lines rather than on analog lines.

ISP *abb.* Internet service provider. Any organization that provides access to the Internet. At its most basic this may merely be a telephone number for connection, but most ISPs also provide e-mail addresses and capacity for your own Web pages.

Java A computer programming language originally designed by Sun MicroSystems for the control of household appliances, which is especially suited for Internet use because it can run on any platform. Java programs can be turned into applets, which can be efficiently transmitted over the Internet to run as small applications in a user's Web browser. Java is thus a useful and powerful tool for Web games and interactive animation.

JavaScript A "scripting" language for applying dynamic effects to web pages.

JPEG, JPG *abb.* Joint photographics experts group. An ISO (International Standards Organization) group that defines compression standards for bitmapped color images. The abbreviated form, pronounced "jay-peg," gives its name to a "lossy" (meaning some data may be lost) compressed file format in which the degree of compression from high compression/low quality to low compression/high quality can be defined by the user, thus making the format doubly suitable for images that are to be used either for print reproduction or for transmitting across networks, such as the Internet, for viewing in web browsers, for example.

Kbps *abb.* kilobits per second. A measurement of the speed at which data is transferred across a network, a kilobit being 1,024 bits.

key frame (1) In traditional animation the key drawings or "extremes" show the position of characters, etc., at the start and finish of a movement or action. These key drawings are done first, and then the in-between drawings are created to complete the illusion of a smooth or effective movement. This concept has been transferred to digital animation and motion graphics in the form of key frames. A key frame is thus a frame whose contents are fully specified (either by drawing or other image creation, and/or by the setting of precise parameters), as opposed to those frames that are interpolated—or tweened—by computation rather than by hand.

key frame (2) A single animation frame in a QuickTime sequence in which information is stored as a reference so that subsequent frames only store changes in the frame ("differences"), rather than storing the whole frame each time, thus making the file smaller. The frames based on changes are called "delta frames" or "difference frames."

keyline A line drawing indicating the size and position of an illustration in a layout.

lossless compression Methods of file compression in which no data is lost (as opposed to lossy compression).

lossy compression Methods of file compression in which some data may be irretrievably lost during compression (as opposed to lossless compression). JPEG is a lossy-compression format.

LZW (Lempel-Ziv-Welch) A widely supported lossless-compression method for bitmapped images. It gives a compression ratio of 2:1 or more, depending on the range of colors in an image (an image that has large areas of flat color will yield higher compression ratios).

Mbps *abb.* megabits per second. A measure of data transfer speeds. A megabit is 1,024 kilobits.

menu A display on a computer screen showing the list of choices available to a user.

midtones/middletones The range of tonal values in an image anywhere between the darkest and lightest, usually referring to those approximately halfway.

mouse event Any input from the mouse occurring at a distinct point in time. Mouse events include pressing and releasing the mouse button, moving the mouse over a specific area of the screen and away again, and so on.

mouse-over The mouse event that occurs when the mouse pointer rolls over a navigation button.

MPEG *abb*. The Moving Picture Experts Group is in charge of the development of standards for the coded representation of digital audio and video. Established in 1988, the group produced MPEG-1, the standard on which video CD and MP3 are based; MPEG-2, the standard on which digital television set-top boxes and DVD are based; and MPEG-4, the standard for multimedia on the Web. The current thrust is MPEG-7, "Multimedia Content Description Interface." Work on the new standard MPEG-21, "Multimedia Framework," started in June 2000. [From MPEG site]

navigation bar A special bar in a web browser, web page, or multimedia presentation designed to help you to "navigate" through pages by clicking on buttons or text.

navigation button A button in a web browser, web page, or multimedia presentation that links you to a particular page.

online Any activity taking place on a computer or device while it is connected to a network such as the Internet. The opposite of offline.

operating system The software (and in some cases "firmware") that provides the environment within which all other software and its user operates. The major operating systems are Microsoft's "DOS" and "Windows," Apple's "Mac

OS" and AT&T's "UNIX," the last three of which all use "GUIs" (graphical user interfaces).

packet A bundle of data, the basic unit transmitted across networks. When data is sent over a network such as the Internet it is broken up into small chunks called packets, which are sent independently of each other.

paint(ing) applications Applications that use bitmaps of pixels to create images rather than the "vectors" that describe lines in drawing applications (called "object-oriented"). Some applications combine both.

parallax The apparent movement of two objects relative to each other when viewed from different positions.

perspective A technique of rendering three-dimensional objects on a two-dimensional plane, duplicating the "real world" view by giving the same impression of the object's relative position and size when viewed from a particular point. The shorter the distance, the wider the perspective; the greater the distance, the narrower the perspective.

pixel *abb*. picture element. The smallest component of any digitally generated image, including text, such as a single dot of light on a computer screen. In its simplest form, one pixel corresponds to a single bit: 0 = off, or white, and 1 = on, or black. In color or grayscale images or monitors, one pixel may correspond to up to several bits. An 8-bit pixel, for example, can be displayed in any of 256 colors (the total number of different configurations that can be achieved by eight 0s and 1s).

pixelation/pixellization The term used to describe an image that has been broken up into square blocks resembling pixels, giving it a "digitalized" look.

plug-in Software, which is usually developed by a third party in order to extend the capabilities of another particular piece of software. Plug-ins are common in image-editing and page-layout applications for such things as special-effect filters. Plug-ins are also common in web browsers for such features as playing movies and audio.

PNG *abb*. portable network graphics. A file format for images used on the Web that provides 10–30% "lossless" compression, and supports variable transparency through "alpha channels," cross-platform control of image brightness, and interlacing.

progressive JPEG A digital image format used primarily for displaying JPEG images on web pages. The image is displayed in progressively increasing resolutions as the data is downloaded to the browser. A cloudy image appears on the screen, which clears as more data is downloaded. Also called "proJPEG."

QuickTime Apple's software program and system extension that enables computers running either Windows or the Mac OS to play movie and sound files, particularly over the Internet and in multimedia applications, providing cut, copy, and paste features for moving images and automatic compression and decompression of image files.

QuickTimeVR QuickTime "virtual reality." An Apple exension that provides features for the creation and playback of 3D objects or panoramic scenes.

185

rasterize(d) To rasterize is to electronically convert a vector graphics image into a bitmapped image. This may introduce aliasing, but is often necessary when preparing images for the Web; without a plug-in, browsers can only display GIF, JPEG, and PNG image files.

raytracing A rendering algorithm that simulates the physical and optical properties of light rays as they reflect off a 3D model, thus producing realistic shadows and reflections.

RealVideo Proprietary streaming video format widely used on the Web, which depends on a plug-in in the user's browser to work.

resolution (1) The degree of quality, definition, or clarity with which an image is reproduced or displayed, for example, in a photograph, or via a scanner, monitor, printer, or other output device.

resolution (2): monitor resolution, screen resolution The number of pixels across by pixels down. The three most common resolutions are 640 × 480, 800 × 600, and 1,024 × 768. The current standard Web page size is 800 × 600.

RGB *abb.* red, green, blue. The primary colors of the "additive" color model.

rollover The rapid substitution of one or more images when the mouse pointer is rolled over the original image. Used extensively for navigation buttons on web pages and multimedia presentations.

server (1) see **client-server**

server (2) A term loosely used to refer to a computer running a server program.

shareware Software available through user groups, magazine cover disks, etc., which is usually only paid for by those users who decide to continue using it. Although shareware is not "copy protected," it is protected by copyright and a fee is normally payable for using it, unlike "freeware."

Shocked The term applied to web pages that contain material prepared with Macromedia's Shockwave technology, and therefore require the Shockwave plug-in in order to be viewed.

Shockwave A technology developed by Macromedia for creating Director presentations, which can be delivered across the Internet and viewed with a web browser.

sprite (1) An object or character that is animated by the substitution of a different image or sprite face for each state, such as the different positions of a waving arm, and the adjustment of its position on the screen. This technique is used widely in animation controlled by computer programming, for example, in Java animation and many computer games.

sprite (2) In Director, a sprite is an instance of a cast member.

sprite face An image that corresponds to a single state of a sprite (1), for example, the different positions of a waving arm in sprite animation would each be represented in a different sprite face.

stop-motion A term often used to refer to the creation of animation by the process of taking a sequence of photographs (on film, video-tape, or direct to disk) of static 3D characters and sets that are slightly moved or altered between frames in order to create an illusion of motion when played back in sequence later.

storyboard A series of small drawings representing key moments, movements, and changes in a live-action film or animation, which are laid out in sequence like a comicstrip in order to convey a sense of the narrative or development of the piece. The drawings are usually accompanied by captions describing the action and sound.

streaming video/audio A method of transmitting video or audio that allows it to be played continuously and apparently in real time. Segments of the received data are buffered while the user's video/audio software plays the previous buffered section.

SVG *abb.* Scalable Vector Graphics. A vector graphics format devised for use on the Web, defined by a World Wide Web Consortium recommendation. SVG images are compact compared with bitmaps, and can be displayed at any size and resolution without loss of quality.

system The complete configuration of software and hardware components necessary to perform electronic processing operations.

TIFF, TIF *abb.* tagged image file format. A standard and popular graphics file format originally developed by Aldus (now merged with Adobe) and Microsoft, used for scanned, high-resolution, bitmapped images and for color separations. The TIFF format can be used for black-and-white, grayscale, and color images, which have been generated on different computer platforms.

tile, tiling Repeating a graphic item and placing the repetitions side-by-side in all directions so that they form a pattern.

tween(ing) A contraction of "in-between." An animator's term for the process of creating transitional frames to fill in-between key frames in an animation.

twenty-four-bit/24-bit color The allocation of 24 bits of memory to each pixel, giving a possible screen display of 16.7 million colors (a row of 24 bits can be written in 16.7 million different combinations of 0s and 1s). Twenty-four bits are required for CMYK separations—eight bits for each.

URL *abb.* Uniform Resource Locator. The unique address of a page on the Web, comprising three elements: the protocol to be used (such as http), the domain name ("host"), and the directory name followed by path-names to any particular file.

user interface The facilities for interaction that a computer program presents to its human users, for example, the desktop interface to an operating system.

vector graphics Images made up of mathematically defined shapes, such as circles and rectangles, or complex paths built out of mathematically defined curves. Vector graphics images can be displayed at any size or resolution without loss of quality, and are easy to edit because the shapes retain their identity, but they lack the tonal subtlety of bitmapped images. Because vector graphics files are typically small, they are well suited to Web animation.

visualization The representation of complex data and information in an easily grasped visual form, for example, an ani-mation showing the evolution of a tropical storm, where wind speed is represented by color.

VRML *abb.* Virtual Reality Modeling Language. An HTML-type programming language designed to create 3D scenes called "virtual worlds."

W3C *see* **World Wide Web Consortium**

Web *see* **World Wide Web**

web page A published HTML document on the World Wide Web.

web server A computer ("host") that is dedicated to Web services.

Web site The address, location (on a server) and collection of documents and resources for any particular interlinked set of web pages.

window Part of the "graphical user interface" (GUI) of a computer, a window is an area of a computer screen that displays the contents of disk, folder, or document. A window can be resized and is scrollable if the contents are too large to fit within it.

Windows Media A Microsoft multimedia format widely used for Web video.

wizard A form of help facility that guides users through tasks, such as the installation of software, or the use of a Java applet.

World Wide Web (WWW) The term given to describe the entire collection of web pages all over the world connected to the Internet. The term also describes the particular type of Internet access architecture that uses a combination of HTML and various graphic formats, such as GIF and JPEG, to publish formatted text, which can be read by web browsers. Also called "The Web" or , less commonly, "W3."

World Wide Web Consortium (W3C) The organization jointly responsible with the IETF for maintaining and managing standards across the Web.

z-order(ing) The stacking order of layers (from front to back) in a program such as Photoshop, or objects in a three-dimensional scene.

189

WEB SITES FEATURED

WEB PAGE CREDITS

Aardman Animations:
© 2001 Aardman Animations Ltd

Amit Pitaru:
Copyright Amit Pitaru, Pitaru Inc. 2000–2001

Babylonheadbox:
Babylonheadbox was thought up and made by Thomas Murphy. Terms and conditions apply.

Bits and Pieces & Noodlebox:

Concept/Implementation Daniel Brown (www.danielbrowns.com)

Belgrade 2001:
Belgrade 2001 was developed, produced and designed by Rob McLaughlin of CBC Radio 3 (www.cbradio3.com). All images and information is Copyright 2001, Canadian Broadcasting Corporation. All Rights Reserved.

Bemboszoo:
© Roberto de Vicq de Cumptich. Website produced by Roberto de Vicq de Cumptich and Mucca Design.

Canal Metro:
Creado y realizado por DoubleYou por encargo de canalmetro, en marzo de 2000.

Claygraphics:
Images Copyright © 2001 Clay M Hagebusch.

Crayola®:
Crayola®, chevron and the serpentine designs are registered trademarks, rainbow/swash is a trademark of Binney & Smith, used with permission.

Dancing Hamsters
Credited to John Zuccarini.

DLX Deluxe:
Blasfem Interactif design the DLXdeluxe Web site.

Exploratorium:
Used with permission © 2001 Exploratorium, www.exploratorium.edu.

Face on Mars:
Face on Mars animations are created by Dr Mark Carlotto.

Flashcan:
Used with permission of Zinc Roe Design. Pages shown were designed by Nathan Jurevicius, Steve Manale and Craig Marshall, with card by Christian Rocha.

Jean-Paul Gaultier:
Website made by Anne Lardeur for ARAGORN and Raphael ELIG for ECHOSYSTEM Paris, 1997–2001.

Go Fuse:
Used with permission of Fuse Interactive.

Japan 2001
Used with permission of Traffic Proximity.

Nofrontierans:
All rights reserved. The Nofrontierans may not be reproduced in any form without written permission from Nofrontiere Design AG.

OpenStudio:
Images of OpenStudio appear courtesy of Andy Deck and artcontext.org.

Once Upon a Forest and Praystation:
Courtesy of Joshua Davis + praystation.com + once-upon-a-forest.com.

Planet 9:
Reproduced with permission of Planet 9 Studios – San Francisco.

Precinct.net:
Precinct.net is produced by Joshua Street Ltd. All rights reserved 1997–2001 Precinct Design Legion/Joshua Street Ltd. The planet and us – together.

SBC:
Designed by Anna-Lisa of Syzygy, produced with permission of SBC.

Sony:
© 2001 Sony Computer Entertainment America Inc. All rights reserved. Used with permission. EverQuest is a trademark of Sony Computer Entertainment America Inc.

Swatch:
Designed by Swatch and is copyright of Swatch Ltd.

Switcheroozoo:
Copyright 2001 Tubehead. All Rights Reserved.

The Forge:
All material © The Forge Studios Ltd., Makers of PoseAmation – Royalty free 3D animation. All rights reserved.

Turbulence:
Empty Velocity was designed by Angie Eng. More-Inc was designed by Wes Meyer. Reproduced by permission of New Radio and Performing Arts, Inc.

wildbrain:
™ & © 2000 Wild Brain Inc. Courtesy of Wild Brain Inc.

Every effort was made by the publisher to secure the permission of all copyright holders.